Employee Body Language

REVEALED

How to Predict Behavior in the Workplace
by Reading and Understanding Body Language

By Harmony Stalter

EMPLOYEE BODY LANGUAGE REVEALED: HOW TO PREDICT BEHAVIOR IN
THE WORKPLACE BY READING AND UNDERSTANDING BODY LANGUAGE

Copyright © 2011 Atlantic Publishing Group, Inc.
1405 SW 6th Avenue • Ocala, Florida 34471 • Phone 800-814-1132 • Fax 352-622-1875
Web site: www.atlantic-pub.com • E-mail: sales@atlantic-pub.com
SAN Number: 268-1250

Library of Congress Cataloging-in-Publication Data

Stalter, Harmony, 1976-
  Employee body language revealed : how to predict behavior in the workplace by reading and
understanding body language / by Harmony Stalter.
    p. cm.
  Includes bibliographical references and index.
  ISBN-13: 978-1-60138-147-7 (alk. paper)
  ISBN-10: 1-60138-147-6 (alk. paper)
  1. Body language. I. Title.
  BF637.N66.S73 2010
  153.6'9--dc22
                            2010014476

PROJECT MANAGER: Crystal Edwards & Nicole Orr
PEER REVIEWER: Marilee Griffin • INTERIOR LAYOUT: Samantha Martin
FRONT & BACK COVER DESIGN: Jackie Miller • millerjackiej@gmail.com
PHOTOGRAPHER: Zachary Bennett • www.Zakbennett.com
MODELS: Harrison Kuo • Marliese Carmona

Printed on Recycled Paper

We recently lost our beloved pet "Bear," who was not only our best and dearest friend but also the "Vice President of Sunshine" here at Atlantic Publishing. He did not receive a salary but worked tirelessly 24 hours a day to please his parents. Bear was a rescue dog that turned around and showered myself, my wife, Sherri, his grand-parents Jean, Bob, and Nancy, and every person and animal he met (maybe not rabbits) with friendship and love. He made a lot of people smile every day.

We wanted you to know that a portion of the profits of this book will be donated to The Humane Society of the United States. *Douglas & Sherri Brown*

The human-animal bond is as old as human history. We cherish our animal companions for their unconditional affection and acceptance. We feel a thrill when we glimpse wild creatures in their natural habitat or in our own backyard.

Unfortunately, the human-animal bond has at times been weakened. Humans have exploited some animal species to the point of extinction.

The Humane Society of the United States makes a difference in the lives of animals here at home and worldwide. The HSUS is dedicated to creating a world where our relationship with animals is guided by compassion. We seek a truly humane society in which animals are respected for their intrinsic value, and where the human-animal bond is strong.

Want to help animals? We have plenty of suggestions. Adopt a pet from a local shelter, join The Humane Society and be a part of our work to help companion animals and wildlife. You will be funding our educational, legislative, investigative and outreach projects in the U.S. and across the globe.

Or perhaps you'd like to make a memorial donation in honor of a pet, friend or relative? You can through our Kindred Spirits program. And if you'd like to contribute in a more structured way, our Planned Giving Office has suggestions about estate planning, annuities, and even gifts of stock that avoid capital gains taxes.

Maybe you have land that you would like to preserve as a lasting habitat for wildlife. Our Wildlife Land Trust can help you. Perhaps the land you want to share is a backyard— that's enough. Our Urban Wildlife Sanctuary Program will show you how to create a habitat for your wild neighbors.

So you see, it's easy to help animals. And The HSUS is here to help.

2100 L Street NW • Washington, DC 20037 • 202-452-1100
www.hsus.org

DEDICATION

To my parents, Regina and Artie, for allowing me to pursue my dream, for your unwavering love and support, and for always being there when I have needed you. I love you.

To my friends for their constant encouragement, support, and for being my lifeline — **I love you all.**

THANK YOU

SPECIAL THANKS to Zachary A. Bennett, photographer; Marliese Carmona, model; and Harrison Kuo, model; for shooting and modeling in a way that portrays body language to its finest.

Without their help, this book would lack the visuals that are essential to understanding the components of body language.

TABLE OF CONTENTS

Chapter 8: Unlearning Behavior Pattern   135

Chapter 9: Nine Scenarios in the Workplace   155

Chapter 13: Getting It Right — Finding Clues About Signals to Make the Right Conclusions   223

Chapter 14: Using Your Body Language to be an All-Star Employee   231

Chapter 15: What You Can Learn From the Masters of Body Language — 245

Chapter 16: Reading Your Own Body Language — 253

Chapter 17: How to Use Your Own Signals to Your Advantage — 261

FOREWORD

By Jeff Reed
Body Language Expert
Investigator — Bureau of Alcohol, Tobacco, Firearms, and Explosives

Imagine if you could have the tools to unlock the innermost emotions of people with whom you interact. Having the knowledge to identify how a person truly feels, despite what they say, is no magic trick. Understanding the meaning behind body language is something that anyone can achieve. Identifying unconscious nonverbal signals and understanding what they mean, when they occur in yourself and others, will help you connect with anyone, anywhere, at any time. Becoming a master communicator through the recognition of body language will allow you to strengthen existing bonds and create new personal and professional relationships, or empower you with the confidence to succeed and win people over in your chosen career.

As a Body Language Expert and Investigator for a Federal Law Enforcement Bureau for more than a decade, I rely on my expertise in body language every day. I have trained hundreds of investigators in the use of body language techniques for interviewing and catching liars and detecting deception. In each and every investigation I have completed, I have utilized my knowledge of body language to find the truth. Through my training, I am able to recognize not just "what" was said, but "how" something was said, which is crucial to determining a person's inner motivation and emotions.

Being able to gauge a person's true emotional state through their body language allows me to adjust my demeanor to appear more like him or her, therefore becoming more "likable." I create positive, open gestures to make the person under investigation feel comfortable and establish commonality. I also use positive body language signals to create a relaxed atmosphere in which people are comfortable to share information and their feelings.

After I have established rapport and trust, when I believe the person is being deceptive, I produce negative signals to challenge a person, intentionally raising anxiety levels. Because no one likes his or her level of anxiety to increase, the person seeks to lower it through easily identifiable "comfort gestures," used to pacify stress. Although I do not recommend purposely causing apprehension within a person in the work place, this gives you an idea of how powerful body language can be.

I have used body language techniques during investigations from simple thefts to bigger scale investigations like the 2002 Washington, D.C., Sniper case. During the D.C. Sniper shootings that gripped the nation and crippled the D.C. metro with fear, ten people were killed and others were critically wounded by shooters Lee Boyd Malvo and John Allen Muhhammed. I used my understanding of body language during interviews of people who came forth with tips about the shooting and judged their honesty. Because people often seek attention by giving false information, an important part of my job is to be able to judge a person's truthfulness. Deception is often the most complex aspect of body language to detect. The key is to look for clusters of deceptive body language signals to begin to identify if someone is being untruthful. Additionally, during this investigation there were many other federal, state, and local law enforcement agencies involved, and I had to earn the respect of others through the use of strong, confident body language. Most know how the Sniper saga ended, and it was the efforts of many people, both the public and law enforcement, that brought the investigation to a close.

There is an advantage when it comes to reading the body language signals of co-workers, which this book guides you through, versus complete strangers. With co-workers, you often have more time to assess their baseline, or normal, behavior and identify when someone deviates from that, which is key to recognizing true feelings. Understanding the body language of your co-workers will open new doors for you, and this book will help you become a body language and communication guru inside and out of the workplace.

There is no more important aspect of interpersonal interactions in the workplace than body language. I call it "Cloaked Communication" because these signals can fly below your senses unless you arm yourself with body language radar. These attempted cloaked communications leak out through many types of calming gestures to pacify stress, and this book will enable you to identify these gestures and understand a person's true feelings.

The information in this book is a practical guide to identifying and using body language to your benefit in the workplace. I use plenty of the information contained in these pages as an investigator, and the same information is known throughout the law enforcement community.

The quote that I think sums up the importance of body language does not come from a scientific researcher or psychologist, but rather from comedian George Carlin who said, "By and large, language is a tool for concealing the truth." In the context of what this book will teach you, that quote can be used to describe the importance of body language in identifying the true feelings of others, because words are often unreliable.

INTRODUCTION

Have you ever wondered what people are actually trying to tell you? Have you ever been talking to your boss and suddenly he or she folds his or her arms and looks away from you? Did you wonder if he or she was even listening to a word you said? Or did you wonder if he or she was mad at you? Have you ever wondered if you were taking too long to explain things? Body language speaks more than words could ever measure. If you "listen" with your eyes instead of just with your ears, you can figure out what people are really trying to tell you. Studies show that body language accounts for more than 50 percent of all communication. If you are good at speaking your mind and making a point, and your words are well received, then you are probably excellent at reading other people's body language. Some people cannot read other people's body language. If you are one of these people, this book is designed to help you.

By the end of this book, you will have a better understanding of exactly what people are saying when they are speaking with you in the workplace. This book will help you figure out how others see you and how to read other people you encounter. You will discover the history of body language and why you need to understand it for everyday work situations. This book will not tell you that everything a person does means something, but it will give you insight into those body gestures that are revealing, and help you learn how to decipher gestures in clusters to unveil the true feelings of your co-workers and employers.

The book is set up to make deciphering body language easy for you. At the end of each chapter, you will find a section called "Did You Catch That?" which will emphasize the key points of the chapter so you can easily review how to present your own body language in the workplace as you communicate with others.

Let us begin by exploring why nonverbal communication exists at all.

Please Note: Everyone is different and some people will be the exception to the traditional rule. This book is meant to be a general guide to understanding body language and the advice within it might not apply equally to everyone. Remember, your situation is unique, so some notes might not apply to you.

CHAPTER 1

Why Does Nonverbal Communication Exist?

Imagine taking a cross-country business trip and getting lost. We have all been there a time or two. You take an exit and suddenly realize that this is not where you wanted to be; your GPS is on the fritz, there is absolutely no phone service, and you do not have a map. Most people would find the nearest gas station in hopes of getting directions back to the freeway.

You see a gas station in the distance, so you make your way over there to ask for help. You push through the front door and once inside, you hope that these people can help you. Looking around, you notice that there are only Spanish-labeled products on the shelves. You do not speak Spanish, so you are not sure if you can communicate where you want to go.

You walk up to the counter and start off by saying "hello" and all the man behind the counter does is nod. You tell him that you are looking to get back on the freeway and go into a rant about how lost you are. Your arms and hands are flailing everywhere, and the man is just staring at you, waiting for you to finish. Once you are done, you are waiting for what seems like forever when he finally answers you with, "No hablo inglés." At this moment, you kick yourself for not continuing Spanish classes in college.

You are frazzled and cannot think of anything other than the Spanish greetings you vaguely remember from class. What do you do? Do you just thank him and leave the store, or do you try to get your message across despite the language barrier? Many people would probably walk out and see if they can find someone else to help — but some will try to communicate with the store operator in hopes of getting directions to their destination. Are you the first type of person, who walks out frustrated and looks for another place, or are you someone who is determined to get your problem solved right then and there by using common body language cues?

Eliminating Speech from the Equation

More than 200,000 years ago, people only communicated with body language and primitive sounds. You can still see people and animals communicating totally by body language. Animals and babies use this form of communication instinctively and are excellent communicators — in fact, body language is often their main form of communication. A baby can tell its parents that it is unhappy without being able to say a single word, but rather by fidgeting, fussing, and crying. Once the process of talking and using words occurs, it is easy to forget about the significance of body language.

You might think that everyone can understand the language you speak and the context you are using. But this is not always true. In the business trip scenario previously described in this chapter, the simplest thing for you to do would have been to write down the name of the freeway you were looking for with a question mark and see if the clerk can give hand gestures to direct you to where you need to go. If that does not work, then body language is your key advantage in this predicament. You can ask to use the phone by just holding your hand to your ear with your thumb pointing straight up and your pinky at your mouth, giving a universal symbol for phone. Before you do this, purchase something so you know your exact location to tell the person on the phone — the address to the establishment you are in will most likely be printed on the top of the receipt. If this works, you can get back on track and head to your destination.

Sometimes, all it takes to break down communication barriers is a few symbols or gestures everyone understands, which is why this book was designed to help you understand the body language of your co-workers, managers, and employees.

Emphasizing Words with an Action

Body language is more widely trusted than the spoken word, and language does not always have to be spoken. If you were to come across an old friend who told you that he or she missed you but did not come any closer, would you believe it, or would you believe a greeting that came along with a huge hug a little more? Although words are still the main form of communication, there is a more developed way to say what is really on your mind — for example, praising your co-worker's presentation, but avoiding eye contact with him or her while you are delivering this praise. This makes body language pertinent in the discovery of what your true feelings are — that the presentation was not really that great — and as a reinforcement of the language you speak.

A study about communication with blind people revealed that, even when talking to other blind people, hand gestures are often used as part of the conversation. This is because from birth, people are taught that speaking with gestures conveys a message better than if no body language is used. In fact, some research, according to the Association for Psychological Science, goes a step further to show that nonverbal gestures are innate from the time humans are born.

This is true for most everyone. For example, most people do not like going to the doctor, but the doctor can do things, without speaking, to make the visit more comfortable for the patient. If a doctor shows genuine signs of interest in the patient's problems, such as leaning forward, not looking at charts the entire time, coming closer to a person, and nodding, then the patient will be less uncomfortable and be more likely to reveal everything that is wrong. The greeting is an important part of the patient-doctor relationship, or any relationship, for that matter. If the doctor comes in with a warm smile and handshake and keeps eye contact during the visit, more concern for the patient is indicated. If a doctor constantly checks his or her watch or looks at the door, these body language clues can make the patient feel like the doctor does not care, or does not have time to listen to his or her problem.

The patient-doctor example can also be used in an everyday work environment. If you go into the office of a colleague or superior and he or she shows the same disinterested body language as the doctor does, you might similarly feel that your co-worker or boss does not have time or interest in your concern. Thus, the line of communication between employees might break down and hinder progress, leaving the issues unresolved. If your co-workers show a genuine interest in what you have to say, then the communication lines will be opened more, resulting in a better work environment. The communication of body language is important in the workplace — it indicates the mood and work ethic of the office.

CASE STUDY: THE SCIENCE OF BODY LANGUAGE

Jeff Reed, body language expert and Federal Law Enforcement Investigator

"I have learned to depend more on what people do than what they say in response to a direct question, to pay close attention to that which cannot be consciously manipulated, and to look for patterns rather than content." — Edward T. Hall, anthropologist

Body language professional Jeff Reed was not always as in tune to nonverbal cues as he is now. After being trained in interviewing, body language, Neuro Linguistic Programming (NLP), and deception detection, Reed has seen the effects of reading body language documented in studies and science in a manner that defines everything that is not spoken — gestures, facial expressions, and posture.

Ultimately, body language is a second source of human communication; a source that is often more reliable or essential to understanding what is really going on, Reed said. People concentrate on the spoken word, which is conscious, and the easiest to control. Rarely do people concentrate on the non-verbal delivery, which is usually unconscious, and thus inherently reveals true meaning.

Research of nonverbal communications shows that people are not very good at masking their true feelings — emotions leak out regularly; in fact, body language cues are given hundreds of times during any given conversation. And yet, the research also shows that most of us cannot effectively decode these cues. Unless you know what to look for, your understanding of the body language cues can be unreliable. But, the more information you can get about the clues you are trying to decode, the more likely you will be to decode them correctly.

The primary effect, as noted by anthropologists and body language experts, shows us that within the first seven seconds of meeting someone, a first impression is made — a statistic that is alarming for a work environment that involves frequent interviews or meetings.

Studies go on to show that individuals retain approximately 20 percent of what they hear, 30 percent of what they see, and 50 percent of what they experience. That alone shows that understanding body language can enhance any interpersonal relationship, because all three elements of interpretation are used in communication.

According to a study by Xerox, only 7 percent of all communication is verbal, with the remainder consisting of non-verbal communication; 38 percent voice tonality and 55 percent body language. Another university study concluded that 18 percent of all communication is verbal, while other studies have shown that between 60 and 80 percent of our message is communicated through our body language, and only 7 to 10 percent is attributable to the actual words of a conversation. Only during intimacy does body language contribute to up to 100 percent of communication, according to author and psychologist Daniel Goleman (1995).

Without body language training, most people rely on their gut feelings and reactions, and not just a reading of the face or a specific body part, Reed said. This is unreliable, but the subconscious is a powerful tool used for understanding why people have good or bad feelings about someone or something.

Simply put, body language cues decipher a person's true emotional state. Studies of the conscious and subconscious by Joseph LeDoux (1996) and Daniel Goleman (1995), show how reactions to questions or situations are processed. The neocortex, Reed said, is responsible for memory, human thinking, and reasoning, and regulates thoughts and controls words used through the brain's editing system. The limbic system, on the other hand, is used for survival, because it regulates the fight or flight response and emotions, Reed said. True emotions are therefore delivered from the limbic system, and are thus responsible for body language cues that are given before the neocortex can edit, or process, them. These emotions, Reed said, are known as micro expressions, and serve as a better measure of truthfulness than the actual words used in a conversation, because emotions are leaked out through facial gestures, hands, arms, legs, and other parts of the body. Paying attention to these parts of the body, and understanding what certain cues mean, will allow you to understand a person's true emotional state, thus enhancing your interpersonal relationships.

The quickest barometer, however, during a conversation, Reed said, is the face because it gives off the most body language cues. But, it is important to note that all cues must be looked at in clusters from all parts of the body to get an accurate read on a person's true feelings. Each facial expression reflects something about the speaker and how he or she is feeling at any given moment, Reed said. "The language of the body not only supplements what we say, but usually dominates our conversation with small gestures, eye movements, facial expressions, and postural changes," he said. For the most part, people know this language; many just do not know how to properly "speak" it. How many times have you audio-logically heard one thing, but visually "heard" another. How many times have you intuitively felt something was not in sync with the words and the body language?

All of the body language cues mentioned above and hundreds of other concepts such as Neuro-Linguistic Programming (NLP) are used in the workplace during every conversation Jeff has.

Body Language:
There's a method for the madness

Neuro-Linguistic Programming, or NLP, is a school of thought detailing the different factors shaping our perceptions. The three key components considered in this way of thinking are neurology, language, and programming. Our neurological system controls the way our bodies operate, while language serves as an indicator for how we communicate with the outside world. NLP delves into the relationship between the mind (neuro) and language (linguistic), offering insight on how this interaction impacts our behavior (programming).

Aside from explaining human perception, NLP creates a belief system about what communication actually encompasses. This school of thought also details the process of change that many people, especially in the workplace, go through. With NLP, individuals have a path to follow for self-discovery. Individuals will have the ability to reveal their identity while uncovering their life mission.

All aspects of NLP are founded on two fundamental ideas. First, humans can never really recognize reality. We can only sense the world around us through our own perceptions of reality. In other words, reality itself does not impact our behaviors, but rather, the way we think about reality, or perceive it, impacts our behavior. We each have our own neurological "map" of the real world, determined by the way we view the actions of others.

The second principle states that processes occurring within and between human beings and their surroundings are considered systemic. There is a connection formed between our bodies, our society, and our universe. As a result, many complex systems and sub-systems are created, which all impact and interact with one another.

Founded by John Grinder and Richard Bandler as a way of constructing models of human excellence, the goal of NLP is to create an extensive map of world perception. The belief behind this school of thought is that the most effective individuals possess a large number of perceptions of their environment. Simply put, NLP contributes to a person's wisdom and ability to read others. The concept of NLP has been implemented in several professions. The tools developed have been influential in creating communication skills, both verbal and nonverbal, and changes in areas such as counseling, psychotherapy, education, leadership, and parenting.

Why You Hide How You Really Feel at Work

There are three major reasons why an employee might not express how he or she really feels at work — groupthink, fear of standing alone, and indifference. These three categories will be discussed throughout this book, because your colleagues and employers will likely fall into one of these groups based on their body language behaviors throughout the day.

Groupthink

Morning or afternoon meetings at the workplace sometimes turn into two to three hour meetings, often due to the employees being unable to reach a decision. Then there are those meetings in which a group of people would rather just agree with what a small percentage of the group says, rather than state their own opinions, in order to avoid arguments. This is referred to as groupthink. If an executive presents an idea, some of the employees might be intimidated and that is when this type of occurrence usually happens. This can be detrimental in how a company is run. If everyone in the company is just a "yes man," then that company is doomed to fail because everyone said yes to both good and bad ideas. Watching the other members' body language will let you know who is just a "yes man" and who really has something to contribute to the meeting. This will also lead to a fear of standing alone.

Fear of standing alone

There is an unwritten rule in the world of business to always make your boss look good. This makes people not want to contest what the executive says, even if it is going to be a bad idea. Most people do not want to stick their necks out. This can cause a tremendous amount of unwanted stress to the employee, which is enough to make him or her never say a word, except to agree with whatever is being said. The fear of standing might make you pass over a great idea that is unpopular at first.

Indifference

There are some people who choose to blend into their surroundings at work, just doing enough to not get fired, but not contributing much value to the company. Some people who seem indifferent might not always agree with what is being said, but they will not state their opinions because they do not want the pressure of seeing an idea all the way through to the end; they remain silent instead. Indifference can be toxic. Some people have become jaded and feel that they cannot make a difference, or they were burned in the past when they stood up for a better idea and were shut down. It can be very difficult to break employees of these habits, unless there is a change in company standards. Some employees who are indifferent might feel like they are being shunned for speaking their minds, unless they are praised for doing so.

Learning to Read

Learning how to interpret the body language of your employees, colleagues, and superiors' body language can be helpful in determining whether or not someone has a better idea but is hesitant to speak, or in determining what is really going on in someone's mind. It can also improve the interactions you have with your co-workers and with people in your personal life. Your business can grow and improve for years with the learning of body language cues, but first, you need to learn the basics of how to read each part of a person's body.

Did You Catch That?

✓ Not being able to articulate with your vocabulary does not mean that you cannot effectively communicate your needs.

✓ Eliminating vocal articulation can make you more perceptive of your audience and your surroundings, therefore making you a better communicator.

✓ Understanding body language in the workplace can help you perceive who may have something to say during a meeting but is not willing to speak up.

CHAPTER 2

The CORE of Body Language

Have you ever left a job interview sure you nailed it, but never got the call back? What about a manager giving you a review and telling you that you are a valuable asset to the company, but then never giving you a higher rating on a job performance report than "good" or "satisfactory?" After going on a sales call to land a new client, have you ever wondered why you did not get the account after you and the client got along well?

By reading the posture, eye contact, and gestures of the person you are talking to, you can decode his or her true feelings toward you. In a business setting, understanding body language can be the most important tool you have. The best example of nonverbal communication is body language. It is important to be a great listener in an office environment, but it is equally important to look for nonverbal clues. Most people are able to understand what is going on in a conversation without hearing everything the other party is saying, just by watching the person's actions. If you are interested in testing your ability to read body language, try this experiment:

Go home and turn on the TV. Find a sitcom with plenty of dialogue between the characters, mute the volume, and watch it. There will be times when you can read the characters' lips, but, instead, pay attention to their posture, how they move their hands around, the amount of personal space between them, their facial features, and the way they enter and leave the scene. Even if you have never seen the show before, you can probably figure out what is going on and how the characters feel about each other based on these clues.

This evaluation can be applied in a work environment, as well. It will take some time to master your ability to read the body language of others, but with the help of the CORE Method of Acceptance (Consistency, Openness, Reaction, and Expression) it can be a little easier. This method will break down the different types of body language and help you to understand how each one works. The relationship between each of these steps and acceptance is important to understand, but first, you should learn what each word means.

C – Consistency

Remember the failed interview you thought you had nailed? Use that as the basis for the explanation of consistency. This means that the body language of the person speaking should match up with his or her verbal communication. In this case, words were spoken, but the body language was inconsistent with what was said. If you are too focused on what is being said, you will miss all the clues held within the body language and facial expressions of the other party.

The failed job interview

The human resources manager may have been agreeing with what you were saying, but did he check his watch, fidget with his cuffs, or flip his pen through his fingers during the time you spent with him?

Translation: He was not giving you his undivided attention and might have been more concerned about another issue than interviewing you.

The Breakdown: If he was checking his watch, he was probably trying to rush you out of the interview so he could accomplish the tasks he needed to finish before the end of his day. If he was more interested, he would have focused on you and what you had to say, instead of on the time.

The fidgeting and pen flipping could mean he was distracted, bored, or even nervous.

If you were able to read this body language, you would have realized that you probably did not impress the human resources manager enough to land the job and could have asked for his honest opinion about your background and skills. This would have given you a chance to clear up any misunderstandings about your background and answer any questions he had about the skills you listed. Your ability to turn the interview around could have landed you another interview. At the very least, it could have provided you with information, from an employer's standpoint, about your strengths and weaknesses, which could potentially put you ahead for your next interview.

The "satisfactory" performance review

Your boss might agree that you were the top performer in the department, but you did not receive any extra recognition. You might not have noticed, but your manager was sending clues that spoke volumes through her body language. She was twisting her necklace, rubbing her neck, looking away from you, and scrunching up her nose while going over your key accomplishment for the year.

Translation: Your manager simply cannot give you an elevated, or excellent, rating, because although you might have been good at your job, you were not exceptional.

The Breakdown: Fidgeting with her necklace or rubbing her neck are usually signs of her being uncomfortable, because she already knew you were receiving the standard, or satisfactory, rating and was not looking forward to sharing the news with you, knowing that you were expecting an excellent review.

Scrunching up her nose says that something might not sit well with her. You may have mentioned that you saved the company millions of dollars this year, and she might not agree with the figure you threw out. Some managers may speak up against your statement, but others will avoid confrontation and show their emotion through their body language — such as your manager's scrunched up nose.

If you were able to read her body language, you would have been able to tell her that you could provide proof for your claims and give her the figures, thus receiving the praise and evaluation you wanted.

Your manager's body language might indicate that she does not want to tell you your review will not be as favorable as you hoped.

The sales call gone wrong

The sales call gone wrong is a favorite of body language interpreters. You left the office on top of the world, because you felt that you really connected with your potential client. You talked about everything and were even offered a golf outing by the end of the conversation. When you presented your proposal, things went downhill from there. You noticed him rubbing his neck and pursing his lips, all while saying the proposal looked great. Now, your e-mails go unanswered and your calls are going immediately to voice mail.

Translation: He might have enjoyed the conversation prior to the proposal, but he cannot afford your rates.

The Breakdown: Once he saw your rates, his body language was no longer consistent with what he was saying. It could have been a great friendship, but business got in the way.

The rubbing of his neck most likely indicated that he was thinking of something to say or trying to figure out a way to clearly express his feelings.

When he was pursing his lips, he was probably telling you he did not like your rates and would not be doing business with you.

If you were able to read his body language, you would have known that he was having a hard time swallowing the cost of doing business with you. At that point, you could have told him the package you were offering was an example of the full package, and you could customize it to suit his company's needs. You would have then gotten a new client for your company, possibly developed a long-term business relationship with him, and might have even gone on that golf outing.

In this picture, your potential client is rubbing his neck and searching for a way out of the deal — his rubbing motion indicates that he is anxious and a bit unsure of the deal you are offering.

The recurring theme in all of these scenarios is that the body language suggests a completely different meaning from the words that are being said — the words and the gestures are not consistent. In using the CORE method to help decipher the body language of those you work with, first see if the hand gestures or facial expressions are consistent with what is being said. If they are, you can conclude that the person you are speaking with is being sincere. If not, you will need to investigate which method of communication is true: verbal or nonverbal.

O – Openness

Once you have an understanding of body language and are able to recognize that verbal and nonverbal communication do not always match, you can then take the reins and change the course of the conversation. This will usually determine just how open the other party is.

If you want to know how you are seen through a different set of eyes, being bold and asking an interviewer for his or her opinion is a great way to get the feedback you need. Using the previous job interview example, if the interviewer is interested, he might give you an honest opinion and point out your flaws, giving you an opportunity to clear up any misunderstandings. If the interviewer has a lack of interest, then there will be a standard reply, such as, "We will be in touch," or "You did just fine." If this is the response you receive and you really are interested in this position, do not let the conversation end here. Continue to ask questions of the interviewer to get more information. Ask if there was something lacking from your résumé to keep you from getting the position. While asking the interviewer questions, make sure to pay attention to his body language.

- Is he shifting in his chair or sitting there calmly?
- Is he leaning back in the chair or sitting upright?
- Are his eyes focused on you or moving around the room?

All these cues will give you an idea as to whether you will be getting the chance for another interview, or even if you have the job. When a person shifts in his or her chair, it means he or she is uncomfortable with how the conversation is going. When people lean backwards, they are usually trying to create as much distance between you and them as possible. If their eyes are darting around the room, then they probably are not open to what is being offered.

With the performance review and the sales call, the same things should be examined. In all three cases, you are seeking acceptance. You want your interviewer, human resources manager, or client to accept you, which is difficult in the professional world of business, but can be rewarding once you have it. It will be easier to receive support from your peers and managers, motivate fellow co-workers, and associate with others when you have their acceptance..

Acceptance – A vital part of any relationship

Back in elementary school, when it was time for team selection at recess or in P.E., there were two types of kids that stood in line. Depending on who you were back then, you either loved the process or dreaded it. The children who were popular, outgoing, and full of energy were always picked first, not the ones who were shy, meek, and quiet. It is the same situation in the workplace. No one wants to be the kid chosen last. You do not want to be left off the meeting list to discuss important projects — you want to be accepted, and the only way to do that is to be open to forming connections. If there is a company picnic every year, go to it and make conversation with as many people as you can. Volunteer to help out on a company outing or go to the Christmas party, but be aware of how other factors, like drinking, influence your body language and attitude. You may want to be known around the office for your good qualities, not for your drunken escapades.

You might volunteer at a company function because you want to get to know your co-workers. But, if you are not really happy about doing it, this may be obvious in your body language and facial expressions, because your body language usually reflects your true emotions. For example, when you smile while irritated, it may look forced because the smile does not extend to your eyes. Your posture might also be slumped in dismay instead of being upright and alert. Your body language will differ depending on how much you drink at the company Christmas party, too. The more you drink, the more you relax your inhibitions. You could show off your dancing skills, or simply be more relaxed with your posture, gestures, and conversation. If you drink far too much, your body language will reflect it — you might sway from side to side or stumble. You definitely do not want to be known for trying to bond with your co-workers this way.

Measures of acceptance

The first measure of acceptance is being accepted by a group of co-workers once they realize that you are not there to threaten their jobs, and you are invited out to lunch or happy hour. This, in turn, leads to the second kind of acceptance in which you are told privileged information. The third level of acceptance occurs when these same people support you at a meeting, or tell you when someone has spoken ill of you. Some people would not put their jobs on the line for the sake of saving their friend, but some will and will even defend your quality of work in order to be able to work with you on a high-profile project.

If you were to invite a co-worker that you had become friends with to dinner after work, this person would most likely be open to the idea. His or her body language would consist of an open stance, a smile, and head nods. However, if you were to invite a person you were just getting to know, he or she probably would not be as open to the idea, even if the person agreed to attend a function with you. His or her body language might consist of crossed arms, shifting eyes, and a fake smile, or no smile at all. By being able to read these body language cues, you will be able to measure your acceptance with your co-workers.

R – Reaction

There are many negative reactions that you can see from the situations previously described in this chapter. Some of those reactions are disdain, shock, pensiveness, and apprehension. These can be seen through body language. You should also be paying attention to the distance between you and the other party and the tone of voice the person is using.

You can use your body language to convey your level of comfort with any situation in the workplace. In the picture above, the exaggerated lean of the female employee generally indicates that she is trying to create space between herself and her co-worker.

Reacting to reactions

You should try to remain positive in professional settings. If you are in a staff meeting that is heading in a positive direction, then it is quite acceptable to mirror the body language of others. If there are smiles and handshakes, then this was a good meeting. If there are frowns and no one really wants to shake your hand, then the meeting did not go as planned. You should still give them kind regards, such as a smile, and thank them for their time. There might be outside reasons contributing to their reactions toward you, so keep the same frame of mind you walked into the meeting with. This type of reaction occurs most during interviews, and it usually means the interviewer does not want to give you too much hope. It may occur when there is more than one candidate for the job and the interviewer or company has not decided who is the best person for the position.

If you use your body language to portray a positive reaction, as well as your tone of voice and demeanor, even the person who did not care for what you were offering him or her will appreciate you a little more, and, it might even result in a second call. Positive body language might not always end in positive results, but people will see you in a more positive light. This can pertain to work and your personal life in the same ways.

Emotion — Taboo in the workplace

Culturally, emotions are not usually displayed in the workplace. Being overly emotional is not seen as being very professional, but showing no emotion whatsoever is not professional either. For example, the carefree receptionist singing to the office's satellite radio station and bobbing her head to the music is immediately seen as unprofessional. However, if the same receptionist were to sit at her desk, still as a rock, this would be seen as unprofessional, too. The co-worker who speaks very loudly to you is probably trying to assert his superiority. Screaming over him would only cause a scene, but backing away from him can show him that you can hear him just fine. You can even massage the outside of your ear to send him a signal that you can hear him. If you answer him while speaking softer, he will probably start to speak softer; now you do not feel like you are being yelled at.

Because of these types of nonverbal signals, Newton's Third Law of Motion is applicable within the workplace. Newton states that there is an equal and opposite reaction for each action. So, when encountering loud co-workers, it is best to respond to them in a quieter tone. By using the opposite reaction, you are creating the response you want. If an excited colleague moves into your personal space, you should increase the space between the two of you. If someone is frowning, smile at them, because after all, smiling can be contagious — just do not smirk at them. A smirk can send the wrong message and hinder your chance of gaining his or her acceptance. Through these examples, you can see how using Newton's Third Law of

Motion applies in the workplace, and how knowing how to react to your co-workers and superiors goes a long way in communicating with them.

Although most employers do not expect you to go through the day without smiling, chatting, or a little laughter, doing these things to the extreme, as shown in this picture, is usually not acceptable. Try to keep your body language and gestures modest so that you do not give off an unprofessional vibe.

E – Expression

The other party's expression will ultimately lead to a relationship or limit the amount of time the two of you will be spending together. Understanding facial expressions and why they are made (consciously and subconsciously) can give you great insight into their thoughts and your acceptance level. *Chapter 3 will delve into decoding facial expressions.*

Do not let them see you sweat ... or cry

The traditional working environment is becoming more modern, making offices, cubicles, and conference rooms less typical. With some careers, such as news reporters, musicians, political figures, architects, and producers, customary standards for portraying body language sometimes get lost outside the four walls of an office, even though these people are still at work. For example, journalists are taught to remain neutral, no matter how tragic the news they are covering. There are times when news anchors have been moved to tears, from being overjoyed or overcome with hurt. For example, during the Sept. 11 tragedies, most reporters near the scene were crying. Similarly, when Barack Obama won the presidency in 2008 there were some reporters in tears— but in this instance they were tears of joy. In both cases, the reporters who tried to hide their emotions through verbal communication, as they pressed on to cover live events and conduct interviews, were visibly overcome with emotions through their body language. You could see them wipe the tears from their eyes as their facial expressions revealed sadness or happiness and their body posture changed. In the instance of Sept. 11, the body posture of some reporters went from an upright, seated position to a slumped position in their chairs with their heads in their hands. In the instance of the Obama win, the posture of some reporters went from being in an upright position with no facial expressions to an even stiffer upright position with big smiles, or a look of shock, on their faces. News anchors, however, tried to remain expression- and gesture-less in both cases.

Expressions tell what the other person is thinking, although, in the workplace, they are usually rare and brief. Many people remain emotionless until it is time for lunch or until they leave the office at the end of the day, when they can speak freely about concerns at work.

The CORE Method for Acceptance Explained

Along with a paycheck, upward mobility, and health benefits, we often seek acceptance in our careers. If your clients accept you, you will probably continue a great business relationship with them. Being accepted by your peers means that they respect you, and if management accepts you, then you might become part of the management team. Think of everyone at your office. Are there individuals who are not accepted? If so, how are they treated? Is it with respect, recognition, or even remembrance? There is never immediate acceptance, but understanding the body language of your fellow co-workers will let you know if they accept you, and let you know just how to interact with these individuals.

You are able to judge the consistency of someone's actions, and how well those actions match up with the words he or she is saying, by knowing just how open the other person is to your messages. You can read the other person's expressions and reactions to determine this. A positive reaction could be them nodding their head in agreement with what you are saying; whereas a negative reaction could be them crossing their arms. A positive expression is a smile, as you are trying to explain something, and a negative expression is the look of confusion on their faces during the same explanation. Variances in body language occur more often than not. For instance, a variance in openness occurs when the other party is nodding in agreement with what you have to say, but is avoiding eye contact with you at the same time. Even when the other party is leaning back and smiling at you, a variance occurs in the person's openness. When a person is leaning back, it usually signifies that he or she is trying to put as much distance between the two of you as the space will allow, indicating that he or she is not happy with how the conversation is going, while the smile indicates he or she is just appeasing you for the time being.

When presenting anything to clients or co-workers, you should quickly determine their openness to your ideas; this way you can change up your approach to make the outcome better. Once you are able to gauge their openness, then you can accurately assess if their body language and words match the message that you are receiving. If your audience is open or closed to your message, then your level of consistency will be at a high point. If you are getting mixed signals, then you will have a low amount of consistency. With a low level of consistency, it will be difficult to determine the impression you are leaving them with.

The sum of all parts

With the CORE Method of reading a person's body language, you can better determine his or her true feelings toward what you are proposing. The purpose of being able to read someone's body language is to understand the level of acceptance you have received with that individual. This means the key to determining your level of acceptance is gauging the level of consistency between his or her verbal and nonverbal clues.

Now that you have learned the about the CORE method of reading body language, you will see that this book is divided into chapters that include body part isolation, along with other cues, like voice tones and touching, to help you to determine your level of acceptance with your peers, managers, and potential clients.

The nonverbal communication identified in this book will not always be applied to every situation; for example, sometimes a person may scratch his or her arm simply because it is itchy. What this book is designed to do, however, is give you the necessary tools to determine what someone is saying to you, even when he or she has not said a word.

Did You Catch That?

✓ It is just as important to pay attention to someone's body language as it is to listen to his or her words in a workplace setting.

✓ Do not focus solely on what is being said, because you may miss body language hints to the true meaning behind those words.

✓ Determining if you have achieved a high level of acceptance comes with the understanding of your peers, managers, and clients' body language.

✓ You can gauge people's openness towards you, and, therefore, be able to adjust your body language to match theirs; this will show them that you understand them.

CHAPTER 3

Tête-à-Tête: Decoding Messages from the
Eyes, Face, and Head

The eyes are a very important part of nonverbal communication. Even if you never see people move a muscle, their eyes will express the meaning and emotions behind their words. If you watch a conversation between two people, you can tell whether the conversation is one sided, intense, or just light chatter.

Everyone has heard the expression "the eyes are the windows to the soul." The eyes are the most powerful feature on your face. As they open, close, fixate, widen, and shrink, they express emotions. They are so expressive, in fact, that often you cannot control what people see in them. People are able to interpret reactions from the eyes better than from any other form of body language. Judges have been known to look into the eyes of the individuals on trial to determine whether or not they are guilty of the accused crime.

This chapter takes you through the difference in eye movements, facial expressions, and head movements — from eye contact to head nodding.

The Importance of Eye Behavior

There has always been a fixation with eyes. Countless songs have been written in tribute to the eyes, such as "Angel Eyes," "Brown Eyed Handsome

Man," "Behind Blue Eyes," "In My Daughter's Eye," and "Starry Eyes." People have even been known to describe others according to what their eyes tell us, coining terms such as bedroom eyes, dreamy eyes, empty eyes, and cat eyes. In addition, many studies have concluded that the most attractive feature on the face are the eyes. The women of ancient civilizations were aware of this and applied makeup to enhance their eyes — a technique still used by women today to dramatize their look.

Magicians are some of the best at understanding the power behind the eyes. Their illusions can fool thousands of individuals. They understand that people rely on their eyes for confirmation, so their optical illusions must be precise. When magicians perform the illusion in which they saw a woman in half, they rely on the people in the audience to see the trick through, using the woman's body language, and believe that the woman is actually being sawed in half. The audience will pay attention to the movements of the woman's head turning back and forth, her screams, and her feet wiggling. When the illusion is performed and magicians pull the table apart, they will ask her to wiggle her feet again, which makes the illusion believable. Then, they close the box back together, open the lid, and take the girl out, revealing her to be in one piece. The audience will then cheer, because what they thought was going to be a dangerous illusion was in fact not dangerous at all. The body language of the woman, however, led the audience to believe the illusion was actually taking place right before their eyes.

Some athletes use their eyes to throw their opponents off by intimidating them. There are times when they will focus their eyes somewhere while running in a different direction, because they know that their opponents rely on clues from their eyes to anticipate the next play. Others use the intimidating, unblinking stare to unsettle their opponents.

Like these previous examples, executives also often use their eyes to powerfully demonstrate or convey their objective in the office. Executives will make sure that they make the optimal amount of eye contact to ensure you understand what they are saying to you. Executives have learned to look directly and deeply into the eyes of their employees, convincing them that they are telling the truth. Understanding how to read other people's eyes can be helpful, no matter what you do for a living.

Proof of intention is mainly in the eyes of the other individual, which is why we rely on the eyes so much. The eyes create a signal that is powerful enough to make you look in the same direction of the person you are talking to, even when no other muscle on that person is moving. In the world of business, the eyes will express meaning that words cannot in certain moments. Therefore, people in a business environment often use their eyes to express their true intentions.

The following pictures demonstrate typical eye movements and what they generally mean. Remember, these movements do not always mean the same thing for every person.

Looking up: a signal of recollection

Looking down and to the left: a signal of contemplation

Looking down and to the right: a signal of emotionalism

Looking straight down: a signal for shame or sympathy

Looking sideways: a signal for uncertainty or hostility

Rolling the eyes: a signal of disinterest, impatience, or disbelief

Along with the direction the eyes are looking, width can play a part in the explanation of the other person's thoughts. Adults are fond of calling children "wide-eyed," because they are so eager to view and experience the world around them. A narrowing of one's eyes often means displeasure, whereas a repeated opening and closing motion, also known as blinking, is a signal of nervousness or dishonesty. Holding the eyes in a closed position for two or three seconds and then opening them slowly typically shows a disinterest in what you are saying.

The eyes do not express emotions alone. The eyebrows work with the eyes and can help in determining the meaning of an expression. Raised eyebrows with an extended stare express disbelief, whereas one raised eyebrow shows that there are some questions about the statements you are making. A brow that is deeply wrinkled might express anger or frustration.

In order to avoid feelings of negativity with your co-workers, looking an individual in the eyes is of the utmost importance while speaking to them.

Some individuals are insecure, passive, or dishonest, and therefore never look another individual in the eyes, and some are just unable to handle the emotions revealed in the other person's eyes. An understanding of the ability to express personality and meaning through your eyes will help you to advance in the corporate world. For a passive person, the power stare is one of the most important things to learn in business. This stare allows you to relay the message that you are confident and important; it is a stare that the other individual is forced to acknowledge.

Eye contact is extremely important when you are making a presentation before a group of individuals. The listeners feel like they are involved, pay more attention, and they will be more alert when they have eye contact with the speaker. Using visual aids during a presentation can be good, but make sure that they are in color and on a screen so that your audience can still look at you and you can maintain eye contact with them throughout the presentation.

If you are going to use visual aids during a meeting, you need to make sure that they are not going to be a distraction, but rather a helpful tool. If they are placed on a screen that you can stand to the side or in front of, then the participants in the meeting will remain focused on what is being said instead of focusing on the visual aids. Making eye contact, especially during a meeting, is extremely important. If there is a decrease in eye contact, your speech might not be as effective.

Strong eye contact during a presentation will help you to engage your audience. You want to portray your authority on the subject through your body language and eye contact.

In this situation, the eyes express confidence and expertise, but that only scratches the surface of the messages that can be conveyed with the blink of an eye. If you are said to have "bedroom eyes," this means that you are sending another person a message of wanting to take them to bed with a half-heavy, lidded look. The term "dreamy eyes" describes when someone looks into your eyes and gets lost in thought. If you have been described as having "empty eyes," then your eyes do not express emotions as clearly as other people's eyes. If you have been told that you have "cat's eyes," then you have an almost opaque-colored eye that is very expressive. This type of eye will convey emotions more easily because of the other person's ability to see the pupil dilation more clearly at a greater distance. Although some of these expressions may not be used in the workplace, they demonstrate how telling the eyes can truly be.

During a presentation, a lack of eye contact with your co-workers, as shown above, might lead them to believe that you are not prepared, are not knowledgeable of the subject, or are not confident in giving the presentation.

Blinking

Research states that on average, a person blinks 12 times a minute, which translates into about 10,080 blinks in 14 hours for a child. For adults, the average can be much higher, especially when body language and facial expressions are used to purposely convey emotions. Blinking even can tell you when someone is stressed or if he or she is lying. If the individual you are having a conversation with is stressed, you will notice an increase in his or her blinking pattern. It does not necessarily mean that he or she is lying to you — blinking can also mean the person is flirting or feeling insecure. Also, people have a tendency to blink more when they are exposed to harsh lighting.

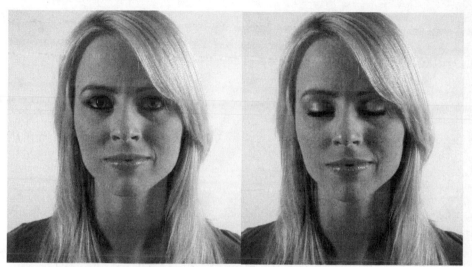

How often do you blink each day? Chances are, you do not even realize when you are blinking, unless you are deliberately batting your lashes.

Eye Contact and Avoidance

Eye contact can be made to show respect to an individual or intimidate him or her. There is nothing that will tell you more than a lack of eye contact, especially in a business setting. When you lock eyes with an individual, it means that you have the person's undivided attention, at least for a few moments. But the lack of eye contact can shows signs of disrespect, submission, or insecurity.

Avoiding eye contact with your co-workers is usually a red flag that something is wrong — you should use a combination of other clues to try to understand what is really going on.

Keep in mind that just because someone is looking you in the eyes, it does not always mean that the person respects you, or that he or she is being honest with you. People who are good liars can easily look you in the eye, say all the right things, and mimic the right body language to persuade you to believe them. But, all you have to do is pay attention to their pupil dilation — that is the one thing that a liar cannot control. When someone is lying, his or her pupils will not dilate at all. People use their eyes for two main reasons: to express interest or intimacy and to communicate power or control over another person. Because of this, eye movements, including piercing eye contact, are used to indicate feelings, and note what is valued, desired, or needed.

The more eye contact you make with a person, the better chances you have of landing that job or account for your business. Between 60 and 70 percent of the time, meeting a person's gaze can help make the other person feel more comfortable with you. It shows the person that you are interested in doing business with him or her, or that you are sincere. When you are the main speaker during a presentation, looking at your audience keeps them interested in what you have to say between 40 and 60 percent of the time, because they are staring at you 75 percent of the time. To do this, it is important that you understand what a stare or a gaze often means.

Shy individuals usually need to work on improving their eye contact methods to help them build lasting business relationships. If a person is shy, he or she might have to work twice as hard to achieve the proper amount of eye contact and maintain that eye contact. The more the shy person makes the effort to engage in the conversation and becomes comfortable with the idea of looking people in the eye, the more the business associate will trust him or her.

When given a chance to work with a shy person who barely makes eye contact, you should make the effort to make that individual feel comfortable through the use of your own eye contact — try to catch his or her eye.

Shifting or darting eyes

When you are involved in a conversation with someone whose eyes are moving back and forth, the person is usually taking in his or her surroundings, and might be looking for a way out of the conversation. This action shows the person is not completely focused on you and might walk away from the conversation quickly.

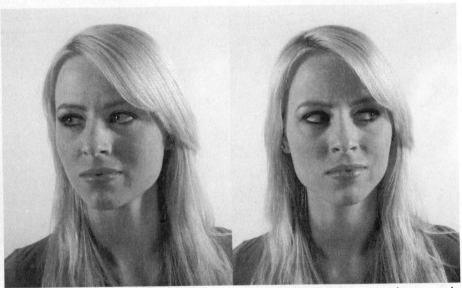

If the person's eyes are darting, or making rapid movements, often unconsciously, it can also mean he or she is uncomfortable in the situation or is distracted by other concerns.

Pupil dilation

People's pupils will tell you whether you are giving them a business deal they like. According to a study conducted by Eckhard Hess, former head of the Department of Psychology at the University of Chicago, if a person's pupils are slightly dilated, then that person likes what he or she is hearing, but, if the pupils are constricted, then the person is not too happy with the way the conversation is going. One thing to remember is that pupil dilation changes with light settings, so there may be situations when the dilation of a person's eyes is not an indication of emotion. If there is dim lighting, the pupils will naturally be bigger. Conversely, the brighter the light, the smaller the pupils. Thus, even though the pupils do not lie, there is no way of controlling how they look.

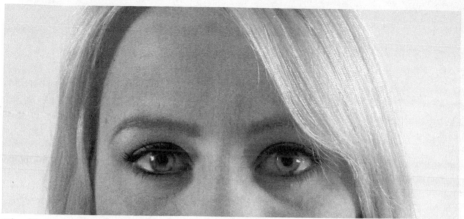

The dilation of a person's pupils can help you determine if he or she is being honest with you in some circumstances.

Face Time

Have you ever had a bad day and, without ever saying a word to anyone, someone asked if you were OK? Most likely, this person picked up on your body language, because it can be very telling in the emotions that you feel. Your facial expressions can reveal what you are thinking, feeling, or expressing at each particular moment. Most of these expressions are done subconsciously, but the muscle movements that occur in your face throughout the day paint a picture of your innermost thoughts. For example, cartoonists use facial expressions to show emotion when there is nothing to say. The cartoonists will do this so the animations take on more of a human form, or to make a joke. The old Tom and Jerry cartoons would use facial expressions to express being scared, surprised, or hurt. Although the main purpose of exaggerating the facial expressions of the cartoon characters was to make viewers laugh, the expressions still conveyed the emotions the cartoon characters were experiencing.

Likewise, the movements in your face are triggered by nerve responses to your emotions and you have no control over them. If you are happy, you smile. If you are upset about something, you automatically frown or grimace, even if you are trying to be in a good mood.

There are six basic forms of facial expressions: anger, fear, disgust, surprise, happiness, and sadness. The emotions of surprise and happiness are typically displayed in the eyes and lower face, while fear and sadness are shown in the eyes. Anger is typically displayed in the forehead, brows, and lower portion of the face. Usually, disgust is apparent in the bottom half of the face. Across the world, however, these emotions can be expressed in different ways, with one exception: the smile. In nearly every culture, a smile is a sign of happiness, agreement, or satisfaction. It is one of the most contagious expressions there is, especially among a group of friends. Once one person smiles in a group, the others usually follow suit.

Within the workplace, smiles are not always a true indication of happiness or agreement. Some people use fake to make you think they are trustworthy or honest. During a business meeting, unless you are greeting others and going over the agenda, a smile is usually avoided. Sometimes, the only acceptable smile during the business day is a toothless smile or a slight grin; this relays that the information being shared is processing and that the other party is paying attention to what is being said. A smile, however, can convey acceptance in the workplace and make it is less stressful environment, but you will not often see the toothy grins you get when you are outside the office. Also, dishonest people do not smile as much as honest people, but when they do, you can easily see that it is a forced smile, indicating their dishonesty.

The eyebrows and forehead will show you when someone it lying or hiding something. Pay close attention to these body signals, especially when someone is pretending to be hard at work. This person may have his or her eyes fixated on the computer monitor or on a stack of papers on the desk, but the person's eyebrows may be elevated in the forehead, giving you the knowledge that he or she really is not paying attention to the task at hand.

In an effort to try to control your emotions, your expressions will not look genuine. For example, when you try to look interested during a meeting you may, indeed, look like you are forcing a stare at the speaker. Similarly, forcing a laugh at a bad joke can come off as a cross between a grimace and crooked grin. But, mastering facial expressions can result in fooling just about anyone. A poker face describes your ability to master your facial expressions, concealing what you are truly thinking or feeling. This is commonly used during card games, and comes in handy when other players are trying to force their opponents out of the game because of the cards they were dealt. This is very common in the workplace, especially when there are negotiations and brokering deals going on.

The best way to master the art of facial expressions is to practice in front of a mirror. It is important to know what your face says about you when you interact with others. While standing in front of the mirror, act out an emotion and study your expression. Then, try to change your expression despite the emotion involved. If you practice this, you apply it in situations where your emotions could directly affect the outcome, especially during interviews, or sales meetings where you have to tell the company that profits are down. The interviewer will not be able to read your disappointment or excitement, and might see you as a future employee, and the company who is losing profits might see you as someone trustworthy who could be management material.

CASE STUDY: A SNAPSHOT OF BODY LANGUAGE

Erin Bisanti, photographer
enbphotography.com

Erin Bisanti is a Daytona Beach-based photographer, where she has photographed the local music scene for a year and a half. As the photographer for Social Menace Clothing, she has worked extensively with body language, trying to position models in particular ways to portray a certain vibe. She has also photographed some national acts that have come through the state and is pursuing her bachelor's degree in photography at Daytona State College.

Bisanti believes if the photographer does not interact with the client, then the tension can create an unwanted vibe while the photo shoot is taking place. When she is trying to evoke an emotion from a client, she gives examples and points out how things like the crossing of their arms may create an unwelcoming feeling for a viewer. Most of her clients are unaware of how they may appear in an image, so by showing them the camera screen and pointing things out to them, explaining the basics of body language, Bisanti can help them feel more relaxed, ultimately allowing them to focus more on how they appear to a viewer.

Being able to tell when a client is unhappy with a shot or when they do not know what is expected of them is important in Bisanti's business, and knowing basic body language cues allows her to make people feel more at ease when photographing them. She finds that humor is often an easy tool to get her models and clients to trust her during a photo shoot. It also helps her elicit unique facial expressions from the clients to make the photo more interesting.

Bisanti believes that the hand, however, is the most forgotten body part. She constantly reminds her clients that their hands are in the shot, reminding them not to ball them up or gesture at the camera. The hands should look like they belong in the picture, Bisanti said. Oftentimes, there are accidental "naughty" pictures, because the hands are misplaced during the process.

Bisanti is just as picky about the positioning of the arms: If you are doing a shoot with Bisanti and cross your arms, she will put the camera down. For lower body positioning, the photographer likes to set up the model or client so there is one leg coming toward the camera, using that body language to create depth for the picture. The legs can flatten an image if the person just stands without addressing the camera, Bisanti said.

In order to create a dramatic effect in her photos, Bisanti will point an individual's chin up at all times while he or she is staring directly into the camera. This will pull the attention to a specific item, like a light in a room, or a body part, like the eyes. The darker the light, like half-shadow lighting or back lighting, the more drama the photo will have. A confident, sharp stance and lighting will create the perfect dramatic scene, Bisanti said.

Head and Shoulders Above the Rest

In the world of business, head placement and movements can mean many different things. It can show what kind of attitude you have toward the task at hand, because it takes the place of spoken words. The slightest shift can be perceived as feelings of interest, dismissiveness, thoughtfulness, arrogance, or anger.

Head tilting

Think of a dog that you might have had either as a child or an adult, and how she would tilt her head in a moment of trying to understand what you were saying. Her ears would perk up, her tail would wag, and her head would tilt from one side to the other. In this moment you know that she is truly listening to what you are saying. Your pets are not the only ones who use head tiling as a form of expression, though.

Head tilting is a common form of expression, although females do it more commonly than males. In the workplace, this can have different meanings depending on the positioning of other body parts, like the hands.

Head tilting is seen as a primarily feminine gesture, but it might mean that you are submitting to the other party and will go along with whatever is being said. This gesture is a sign of submitting because you are exposing your neck. Think of a vampire film where the woman willing for the bite exposes her neck to the vampire, thus submitting to him. This nonverbal signal can directly translate to the workplace. During a meeting, female executives need to be aware that their heads will cock themselves this way subconsciously and should try to control that action, even when they are in agreement with their male counterparts, because head tilting is a sign of vulnerability. The first movement involved in head tilting is exposure of the neck, which makes you appear as though you are submitting, or appear that you are straining, or trying, to understand what the other person is saying. In the business world, you do probably do not want to appear vulnerable. But, when you complete the second motion of a head tilt, a slight tilt to the right, you can give off the vibe that you are trustworthy, or that you are sincerely trying to understand what the other person is saying to you. This can be particularly helpful during an interview or when meeting a new client. If you are giving a presentation, look for this type of tilting with a forward lean with one hand placed on the chin — you will know you are getting you point across if your colleagues or audience is mimicking this language. If the person speaking tilts his or her head to the left, then he or she is looking for sympathy. When a person tilts his or her head to the left while speaking, it is generally an involuntary motion that probably indicates he or she is upset about something. This motion makes the other person in a conversation feel an outward emotion of sympathy toward him or her.

Head shifting

When people are feeling uncomfortable in a situation, they will usually shift their heads away from the party they are interacting with. This is a way of creating distance between themselves and the individual. Watch for the following head shifts:

- Abrupt jerk backwards
- Slow withdrawal

The abrupt jerk backwards can indicate a state of shock about what is being said, but can also mean that this person is trying to quickly create as much distance as possible between the two of you. The slow withdrawal, on the other hand, probably means that this person is not liking where this conversation is going or is trying to leave the conversation. Because this person does not want to offend you, he or she will shift the head slowly to distance himself or herself from the conversation. Both of these shifts are typically signs of discomfort.

The head duck

The head duck occurs when someone is walking with his or her head lowered between the shoulders. This gesture is one of submission, and often times can be seen when someone is approaching the boss' office. This might means that he or she is not confident in the meeting about to take place. It can also indicate the relationship status between the two individuals. There will be times when a manager is talking to a subordinate or when the subordinate is being reprimanded. The subordinate will duck his or her head, as if to avoid a confrontation. Often times, you will see this when two people are in a conversation and a person walking by might not want to intrude on their personal space.

There are many forms of the head duck, but you will sometimes see it when a co-worker or employer is trying to avoid you. This upper body posture is also used to convey feelings of insecurity.

Holding your head up high

Someone who is showing confidence will hold his or her head up high. But, someone with a low level of confidence will hold his or her head at a lower level. This can give off a neutral attitude towards the words that are being spoken. If the chin is forward, then that person is stating that he or she is superior, fearless, or arrogant.

When individuals rest their head in their hands, it typically means that they are considering what you have to say. If they lean back in their chairs while doing this, then they could be bored with what you are saying, but if they are leaning forward, then they usually are genuinely interested in what you have to say. When people are sitting at their desks with their heads in their hands, then it could be that they are tired over what the work day has

Hold your head up high or having a jutting chin can appear as an attempt to gain height or make others look down at you.

brought to them or dealing with grief. Either way, these people are having trouble concentrating on what they are working on.

Head nodding

A nod of the head is perhaps the most important of all head gestures used in the business world. These indicate that you are listening to the person speaking and that you agree and are encouraging them to continue. This gesture is seen as positive; although, the person listening might not always be in agreement. With a head nod, you can at least tell that he or she is showing an interest in what you are saying.

Sometimes, the individual can excessively nod the head, which might mean he or she would like you to hurry up, often so that he or she can have a turn at speaking. Generally, the fast head nod show signs of impatience, whereas the slow head nod shows an interest and understanding in the other person. If you have positive feelings, then your head will automatically nod. Likewise, nodding your head more often will help you to feel more positive. Head nodding, like smiling, can be very contagious. If the individual you are communicating with nods at you, you are likely to begin nodding along, too.

Did You Catch That?

✓ Other peoples' intentions are expressed through the eyes.

✓ If you trying to advance in the workplace, understanding your ability to show emotion and meaning through your eyes is the key.

✓ Your facial expressions show what you are feeling, regardless of your desire to show your feelings.

✓ Anger, fear, disgust, surprise, happiness, and sadness are the six universal facial expressions recognizable to everyone.

✓ Head positions and movements tell the individual if you are interested in what he or she has to say.

✓ Head nodding is one of the most common gestures in the workplace and has many meanings.

CHAPTER 4

Arm Wrestle: Everything You Wanted to Know
About Arms and Hands

U sing one's hands and arms to talk is part of the evolutionary process. Humans went from strictly using body language to making grunting and groaning sounds to using speech, which, combined with our body language, communicates our messages to other individuals today. This is a natural thing to do, and it is not easy to grow out of.

People have been molded since childhood to put up defense mechanisms to protect themselves from unwanted advances. This is more apparent in the business world, where you are more likely to be scrutinized for a botched job, than in other areas of life. If you mess up an important account, you can expect to be in the boss's office the next day being reprimanded. If your idea or campaign pitch did not turn out to be profitable, then you might be chastised at the next meeting. Therefore, you might resort to using your arms as a barrier against these unwanted advances.

When displayed in certain positions, your arms can hold significant meaning. This chapter will discuss everything about arm positions and hand movements, from crossing your arms to twisting your hands.

Crossed Arms

Crossed arms can usually be seen in two ways: a comforting gesture or a defensive gesture. In a work setting, crossed arms usually indicates the latter; you are closed-minded about what someone is saying to you. This is seen as the worst of the worst negative stances. The person doing this in a business meeting is probably disagreeing with what you have to say or is no longer paying attention, and there are statistics to prove it. A person who crosses his or her arms while listening to a speaker retains up to 38 percent less information than a person who sits with his or her arms resting comfortably at his or her side. Aside from using the arms as a barrier to ideas and information, some people cross their arms when they feel insecure, apprehensive, intimidated, or anxious.

If you are standing in a group of people and one person has this stance, it is likely others will follow suit. Once everyone in the group has done this, it is difficult to get the group to revert back to an open stance. There are different types of crossed arm gestures and each one means something different.

Did you know that crossing your arms can actually mean that you are paying less attention? By closing off your upper body, you are reducing your ability to take in information.

Gripped crossed arms

When someone has his or her arms folded across the chest, gripping the arms, it is a sign of anxiety and apprehension. This person gives the impression that he or she is holding on for dear life. Some people grip so tightly that their knuckles turn white. You can see this position often in a doctor's office, and it is a signal that this person is nervous and needs reassurance.

Crossed arms with clenched fists

If you cross your arms and clench your fists, you may look like you are heading to a fight. This particular position can be viewed as hostile and used as a defense mechanism at the same time. It can easily lead to an aggressive behavior pattern. This particular version of the crossed arm stance can also show a position of authority and control. This position is often used by police officers to demonstrate that they are in charge and to establish authority in any given situation.

Crossed arms with thumbs pointing upward

Primarily used by young, up-and-coming men, this arm position is used when dealing with a superior. This position gives off a sense of apprehension, but still portrays confidence. The crossed arms, in this position, shows that the person is uneasy, but the thumbs show that the person still has good self-esteem. The cool and under-control vibe that the upward thumbs convey can be confusing when utilized with a superior, because it conveys apprehension and confidence at the same time.

If you are speaking with a person who suddenly folds his or her arms, you probably have said something he or she does not agree with. In order to turn this position back into a receptive state, give the person something to hold or do with his or her hands. The person will be forced to change his or her body language and pay more attention to what you are saying. It is pointless to continue your presentation, negotiation, or conversation when someone has crossed his or her arms, because that person will no longer be listening. The key is to figure out what the person disagrees with and get him or her to change his or her body language to an open stance, which will foster an open mind.

Hidden Arms

Think back to your childhood days when you would see people with their arms behind their back asking you to pick a hand. Usually the objective of the game was to find the hidden object. The initial gesture, with the arms behind the back, meant the person was hiding something, until he or she brought out both hands, asking you to choose which one the object was in. In adulthood, and more specifically the workplace, hidden arms during conversations still carry the same meaning. When people have a conversation and they suddenly hide their arms behind their backs, they usually have something to hide from the people they are talking to.

What is she hiding? Placing your hands behind your back could be a co-worker's first clue that you are keeping something from him or her.

Say you are talking to a superior about a project and something had gone wrong, but you are afraid to tell your boss; your arms will suddenly go behind your back. You might be afraid to tell your boss that the project was not completed, or that the client you were sure that you had landed decided to go with another company. Your hesitance to reveal these types of information can make your arms involuntarily go behind your back, and your boss might realize you are hiding something just by reading your body language.

Hidden arms can also be seen between a man and woman as a means of flirtation, but only if you see them with their heads tilted to one side, they are smiling, and/or have a hand in their pockets. When you see a man and a woman standing together and either one has his or her head slightly tilted to one side, and they are particularly engaged in their conversation, they are conveying interest in the other person. They are smiling to express that they are open to what the other person is suggesting. The key signal for flirtation in this situation is their hands; they will usually be in their back pockets or behind their back, exposing their torso.

You will also see this position when people are trying to apologize for something without actually having to say the words. They will have their arms behind their back, possibly with one hand grasping the elbow of the opposite arm. Picture a child who has done something wrong, but does not want to admit it; the child will take this stance, but will probably swing his or her body from side to side while denying what he or she is being accused of. The difference between a child taking this stance and an adult is the adult has typically given up the swinging of the body.

Having the arms behind the back, with one elbow clasped, will also show a person's insecurities, while indicating the person is not trying to put up any barriers to ward off someone else. An insecure person will usually look down or away from the other person, too.

If you see people walking with their hands behind their backs and clasping one wrist, they are showing authority and confidence. Picture your boss strolling around the office this way, checking on the employees and their progress on the day's work. By doing this, he or she is leaving his or her torso open to subconsciously show the other people in the office that he or she has all the power. Aside from bosses and top-level business executives, this stance is also seen in political figures and school heads or teachers. These types of people will usually have a neat appearance and command respect, especially through their body language.

The clasped hands behind the manager's back are showing his authority in this picture, as he checks on his employee.

Shaking Hands Motions

How you shake someone's hand says plenty about you as person, especially in the business world. The handshake conveys a bond between the two parties involved. It can cement an agreement, offer a welcome, or bid someone a farewell. You must convey this gesture with a positive, open attitude. Deciding which person advances his or her hand forward first is a key element. Typically, this gesture is done when first meeting a person, but if that person is immediately uncomfortable meeting you, it can be awkward. If you see this person as your equal, then extending your hand first should not be a problem. In the business context, some people are unsure as to whether they should shake a woman's hand, so she should extend her hand first to show that she is comfortable with shaking hands. There are many types of handshakes, and for each, there is a time and a place.

The bone cruncher

The bone cruncher tells you that the other person is overly aggressive and is compensating for something. This type of handshake will hurt your hand. The person that executes the handshake might not know his or her own strength or might not have very good social skills. There is nothing you can do to counteract this type of handshake, other than letting the person know he or she hurt you, especially if you feel that it was done on purpose.

With a tight grip and a big forward lean, this male employee is using the bone cruncher hand-shake. By the look on his client's face, she is unimpressed with his eagerness or over-exertion of power.

The wet fish

This handshake sends the message that you are timid, insecure, or nervous. This is one of the most unappealing handshakes out there — the palms are moist and there is a lack of commitment. The people who execute this handshake can appear self-conscious and aloof.

The female employee is hesitant to shake hands with her sweaty-palmed co-worker.

The power shake

In order to execute the power shake, your hand should be facing the downward position. This shows the other person that you are the one in control of the situation because your hand is on top. In this particular handshake, the person with the downward palm is dominant. This is a firm handshake used to let the other individual know that you, the person executing the handshake, wants to be in control of the situation. If you are on the receiving end of this handshake, counter it by giving your wrist a slight turn so that your thumb and the other person's thumb are facing the same way. If the person resists, then he or she just might want to dominate the task at hand.

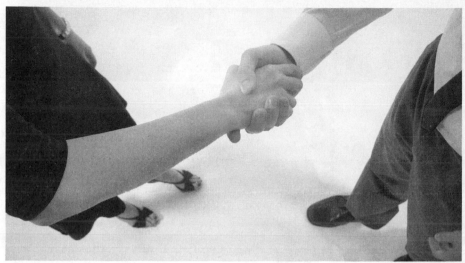

In this picture, the employee with her hand on top is taking control of the situation and exercising power.

The male co-worker did not receive the power shake well. This picture shows his attempt to balance the power, as he has managed to turn both of their palms to a vertical position in spite of his co-worker's resistance.

The glove, double hander

Using your free hand to cup the hand of your co-worker, client, or superior can make for a true and genuine greeting. This type of handshake works best when used with someone you already have a business relationship with.

Politicians and corporate leaders favor this particular handshake. When the other person reaches out his or her hand, this shaker will cup the hand with both hands, in an attempt to display sincerity, honesty, and deep feelings toward the other person. You increase your physical contact by using both hands, showing the other person you have the upper hand. If this handshake is done when first meeting a potential client or new contact, it can have the reverse effect on the person receiving it. The person can become suspicious of you or your intentions toward him or her. It can seem as though you are trying to invade his or her personal space, or as though you are trying to control the situation. This is an overly affectionate handshake and should only be used for people you already know.

The firm handshake

This handshake conveys a sense of equality. The palms of both parties are vertical and meet in the middle. Women often favor this handshake in a business setting, because it lets the men know they feel they are their equals and are up for a no-nonsense meeting of the minds.

This is one of the most commonly used handshakes, because the vertical positioning of the hands means that neither party views themselves as superior or more powerful; this is a strong, but neutral, handshake.

The stiff arm

Aggressive people usually use this type of handshake. The types of people who will execute this handshake want to keep you as far away from their personal space as possible, and they will protect that space at all costs, even if it means locking out their joints to create more distance during a handshake. The people who use this form usually come off as distrusting, aloof, or reserved. There are times when the person with the stiff arm will even lean forward to do this handshake as a way of keeping you even further from his or her space. By leaning forward, the person is actually forcing the other individual to take a step back, thus creating a larger space between them.

A stiff-arm handshake is commonly used to protect personal space. Keep in mind that using this handshake may make you appear standoffish.

As seen in the picture above, placing the free hand on another person's body will bring you closer to him or her, closing the distance between you and invading his or her space.

The space invaders

These are the people who automatically shake your hand and place their other hand on your arm or shoulder, invading your space. They are usually trying to tell you that they are the ones in control. But, if you thrust your hand forward and then bring it back to you, pulling the other person into your space, you are letting that person know that you are in charge. The people who execute this type of handshake usually seek power and control. You might see this used by the managers of a company with their insubordinates or when a business meeting with a new client is about to take place.

Tips on Creating a Positive Message — How to Use the Eyes and Hands Together

A good handshake is important for any business encounter — everything from your smile and eye contact to the strength of your grip will influence how the other person perceives you.

- Always look the other person in the eyes while shaking hands
- Smile
- Stand up when you are being introduced and shake the other person's hand
- Always make sure your right hand is free for shaking — shift everything else to the left side before approaching the other person
- Face the other person — never angle your body
- Make sure there is palm to palm contact and the webs of your hands meet
- When offering your hand, make sure it is in the sideways position to create a sense of equality

- Always use a firm handshake, especially if you are a woman, to show equality and power
- Keep a grip on the other person's hand for a few seconds longer while you exchange greetings to show sincerity
- Always talk before you let go so the handshake is not abrupt
- Avoid looking down when you break away to portray confident, open communication

Clasping Hand Motions

The hands are second in importance only to the face in regard to expressing emotion. They can help you get your point across in one motion. The way you position your hands tells a person your intentions toward him or her.

Folding the hands can be a symbol that you are trying to remain poised or calm, especially during a business meeting. In some instances, though, it is also used as a courtesy while someone is speaking.

Folded hands

This is often seen as a negative gesture, because it usually relays your frustration to the other person. It also tells the person that you are holding on and not letting go, sometimes in a hostile manner. If a person is frustrated with the person speaking, you will see this gesture being used. When you attend meetings and someone is not allowing other parties to speak, you will probably see this throughout the room, often until that person gives someone else a chance to get a word in. This hand position will also occur if the meeting is not going well. The other members will have folded hands until given their turn to speak, possibly signaling that the members waiting are impatient and annoyed that they are unable to talk.

Hand clenching

There are many different variations of this particular motion. How you see it being used depends on the message the person is trying to send. Generally, the hand clench signifies a nervous feeling or shows that the person is scared or holding back a negative emotion. The placement of the hands is the key to what the true meaning is.

Holding the hands in a higher position, such as right in front of the face, often reveals a strong negative mood. When dealing with your boss, if his or her hands are by the mouth in a clenched fashion, it will likely be difficult dealing with him or her. When the hands are clenched at the higher position, the level of frustration or annoyance is probably at its peak.

With both hands clenched together, irritation is evident. When combined with other nonverbal cues, such as the eye roll, clenching the hands in front of the mouth immediately conveys a negative attitude.

The positioning of this employee's hands conveys a different feeling from the preceding picture. Here, her hands are lightly clenched, or laced, together, indicating a more relaxed, open mood. Also, holding her hands at the midway point opens her body language more than if her hands were raised high. This is appropriate body language for listening during a meeting.

The fig leaf is a common protective stance in the workplace. Though some body language remains open, with wide legs and a relatively open chest, the folded hands close the body language off.

At the midway point, however, clenched hands mean that the other person is annoyed at the situation taking place, but has not yet reached the breaking point. Both of these clenched hand positions occur when the person's elbows are resting on a desktop or table. People also sometimes stand with their hands folded in front of their groin. This position is commonly referred to as the fig leaf. This stance is usually a sign of people looking to protect themselves, because they feel threatened.

The steeple

The raised steeple occurs when the fingers are in front of the chest and the speaker is relaying his or her thoughts or opinions. This motion displays confidence in a person. On "The Simpsons," the character Mr. Burns often creates the steeple position while he is plotting. He is showing off his confidence level. If you take this position to the extreme, you can come off as arrogant, like Mr. Burns. If you happen to tilt your head back while utilizing this position, you will probably be seen as arrogant or smug. The lower steeple, where your hands are in the downward position while in this form, shows that you are listening and interested. The fingers will either be in the downward position, or the hands will be at the chest, straightened with only the fingertips touching each other.

Placing your index fingers and thumbs together, and weaving your other fingers, creates the steeple position. This hand position can take on various meanings depending on where the hands are in relation to your body.

Twisting Hand Motions

Rubbing your hands together can give off a positive expectation. The pace of your hand rubbing determines who the beneficiary will be at the end of the interaction, you or the other person. The slow hand rub means that you are not faring well in a situation, whereas a fast-paced one means there is excitement, pleasure, and enthusiasm, and you are doing well with the proposal you are giving, or receiving.

For example, a co-worker may come up to you and tell you she is excited about an upcoming event in her life; while she is talking, she may rub the palms of her hands together in a fast-paced manner. This will indicate her excitement for the project. In other cases, people may twist their hands while negotiating a deal. If it is in a fast motion, it usually indicates they are receiving the biggest benefit from the deal. If the person negotiating the deal is rubbing his or her hands in a slower motion, then he or she likely has a bad feeling regarding the outcome of the negotiations.

The hand twist can also be used to show someone, such as a villain in a movie, who is plotting his or her next move. This move is normally accompanied with an evil laugh. The person will rub and twist his or her hands

Rubbing or twisting the hands can also be a symbol of anxiousness or nervousness, depending on the circumstances and other body language cues. In the picture above, the employee appears nervous.

together, signaling that the plan is in the process of being hatched, and the villain is sure he or she will succeed.

The precision twist

This grip reinforces what you are trying to say. Place your thumb and forefinger together and face your palm upward to show the listener you are using accuracy and precision to reinforce your statement. This type of positioning can also be known as the politician point, where the fingers are rounded softly and pointing outwards.

The precision twist gives the perception of being thoughtful and goal-oriented.

The power twist

Strong, serious, and powerful people use this gesture to make a point. There are two ways of using this gesture effectively. The first occurs when you are delivering a message; leave your fingers loosely closed. This is a way of gesturing without touching anyone. The hand will be balled into a loose fist while the person is making his or her point. The second way tells the other person that you mean business, and is shown by having your fist completely closed. With this gesture, the hand of the person speaking will be balled into a tight fist and there might be some pounding on a table.

Whether the fist is tight or loose, the power twist is used to portray authority and make a strong point.

The power chop

In this motion the hand is moved like an axe blade. This shows the listener just how important your point is to you. If you disagree with the other party, you can stop them from talking by using the double chop motion, which includes your arms being crossed in front of you and moving your hands back and forth.

The motion of the power chop conveys your authority and seriousness for the subject you are speaking about.

Did You Catch That?

✓ How your arms are displayed can make you appear to be on the defensive.

✓ The handshake is the most powerful bonding tool In the business world.

✓ Hand positions and movements can demonstrate the point you are trying to get across.

CHAPTER 5

Can't Keep Running Away: Leg and Foot Movement

Our brains control our legs in the near-instantaneous reactions of freeze, flight, or fight. Your stance can tell the other person just what you are thinking and feeling. From the way you stand to the way you sit, your leg and foot positions can say much about how you are feeling. The signals being sent by the positioning of your lower extremities is significant in how you receive and send signals to the opposing party. The signals your legs and feet show include:

- Anxiety
- Anticipation
- Welcome
- Exclusion
- Interest
- Retreat

By the end of this chapter, you will be able to spot all of these in your next meeting with the board, a client, or your boss.

All About Your Legs

There are two different leg positions — open and closed. The further the body part is from the brain, the less aware we become of what it is doing. An open position of your legs can show dominance, relaxation, a high comfort level, and confidence. The crossed position might show a closed attitude and uncertainty, except for in the case of women, who tend to cross their legs when in a natural seated position.

Legs crossed

This can be the most comfortable position while sitting down. The meaning of this leg position depends on whether or not the legs are outstretched and crossed at the ankles or are crossed at the knee. If the legs are outstretched and crossed at the ankle, this usually signals the person is at ease and very comfortable.

As one of the most common leg positions, you will see the legs crossed often in the workplace.

The European leg cross

This is the standard way of crossing your legs. One leg is crossed over the knee of the other leg. If the person crosses the hands, he or she might be signaling that he or she is completely closed to the conversation. People with closed body positions have a tendency to talk in shorter sentences, reject more proposals, and overall do not remember as much of what is said at meetings. If you are meeting with your boss, client, or co-worker and this position is how the person starts the conversation, you might not be getting through to him or her. If this is the case, you might try to get the person to change leg positions. Perhaps suggest a different office setting, or a walk to your desk where you can give a last-minute visual to support your conversation. This way, the person you are speaking with will be forced to move out of the European leg cross, and hopefully will change positions when it comes time to sit down again.

Because this leg position is so common, look for other clues, such as the direction of someone's body or the amount of eye contact, to tell you if conversation is welcome.

The American figure four

This position consists of you placing your left or right ankle on the opposite thigh, right above the knee. If you were to stand in front of a mirror and attempt this position it would look as though your lower body has made the number four. This can give the perception of dominance, or show that the person is relaxed and youthful, as demonstrated when the motion is performed as a stretch after exercising. Because it highlights the genital area and is usually seen as an argumentative or competitive way of sitting, this position is mainly used by men. Most women do not sit like this because they do not want to seem too masculine or come off as sexually available.

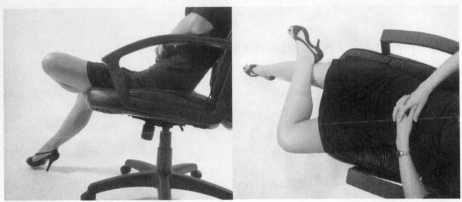

This position, commonly used by men, indicates comfort and control. Although many women will not sit like this in a business setting, this seated position can be used when a woman is trying to express equality with a male counterpart.

The additional clasp of the hand to the ankle could mean that your co-worker or employee is ready to confidently object to what you are about to say.

The figure four leg clamp

This is a variation of the figure four, in which at least one hand is clamped on the crossed leg. This projects the person as strong-willed and stubborn. This person will more likely reject others' opinions. When encountering a client or superior in this position, be careful, and tread lightly to avoid an argument.

The leg twine

When approaching a client or co-worker sitting like this, be friendly in order to open this person up to you.

This sitting position occurs when a person locks the top of one foot behind the opposite leg. It can indicate an insecure attitude and is typically used by shy, timid women.

Standing Leg Positions

The way you stand, often referred to as your stance, can tell a person how to approach you, what attitude you are going to have toward what they say, and your level of commitment to the conversation. There are many ways we stand and present ourselves to the world, but the most common stances are outlined here.

When you are standing at attention, you are alert and ready for whatever comes your way.

At attention

This stance gives a no-commitment attitude and is used every day, unless we are feeling some sort of emotion toward the other person. You are standing with your feet together and hands at your side, or sometimes behind your back. In the armed forces, you will see all military personnel stand at attention. They will have perfect posture, sometimes with their hands at their sides.

Straddle stance, legs apart

In this position, the feet are placed evenly apart, distributing the weight equally between both sides. This is mainly a standing position used by males, but some females are known to stand like this, too. Depending on how your upper body is positioned, the meaning can differ, sometimes severely. For example, if the person standing in this position has his or her hands on his or her hips or the arms are crossed, do not approach him or her. They will most likely be cold toward you.

This position is all about power displays, especially when combined with certain upper body gestures like crossed arms or placing the hands on the hips.

This position is common when having a standing conversation with a co-worker, but be careful to not just pass this off as the way someone stands — the person could be trying to leave the conversation, or could be reacting to an uncomfortable situation.

Buttress stance, one foot forward

This position requires one straight leg, and one leg to either be bent or straight but pointing in another direction. All the weight is placed on the perfectly straight leg, but if you see that person shifting his or her weight to the other leg, that person could be trying to tell you he or she is done with the conversation and would like you to leave.

The crossed position of the legs means that your co-worker, boss, or client is anchored to his or her spot and is listening to what you have to say, but not completely open to your ideas.

Scissors stance, legs crossed

This position is much like the outstretched legs crossed position, but done while someone is standing — which has a totally different meaning. This position can convey negativity, defensiveness, insecurity, commitment, immobility, and submission. Someone standing in this position will not take flight and leave in the middle of a conversation. The person wants to be there, but might feel the need to be defensive because he or she is insecure while in the company of the person speaking.

What Are your Feet Saying About You?

The feet are a primary indicatory of a person's honesty. No matter how much the person can control his or her facial expressions and upper body movements, the feet will not remain still. When someone is lying, the increasing foot movements are a dead give away as to just how deceptive the person is trying to be. But, lying is not the only thing that feet positions or movement can uncover.

Fidgeting feet

When you see someone with fidgeting feet, it could be a sign of impatience. These people might be indicating that they want to run away and are unable to. During a business situation, if the person has been constantly bouncing his or her feet but stops after the offer is off the table, the foot fidgeting was probably in anticipation of the deal. If the feet are only moving at the end of a conversation, then the person likely is ready to take off, because he or she probably does not like how the deal is being negotiated.

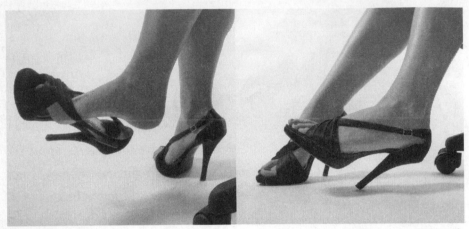

Fidgeting feet can also be a sign of boredom, nervousness, or anxiety. Just because this might occur under the conference table does not mean that your managers and co-workers will not notice.

Knotted ankles

Twisting your ankles together is referred to as knotting your ankles, which gives the perception of a closed off space, insecurity, ambiguity, lack of confidence, and a negative attitude toward what is being said. There are instances when people say they are just comfortable sitting like this, and it may be true, but it could be their frame of mind that associates this position with comfort. Most people will knot their ankles when they feel left out, or if they are holding back something important.

Pay attention to the positioning and looseness of the ankles to see how your co-workers are feeling. Knotted or twisted ankles could mean that the person is uncomfortable.

If you are sitting across from an executive that has crossed her legs, pay attention to the foot position. If the foot is pointing toward you, then what you are saying is being received, but if the foot is pointing the other way, she might be done with the conversation and want to leave. An easy way to find out if you can join in on a conversation that two of your colleagues are having is by paying attention to the direction of their feet. If the feet stay pointed away from you, then you are not invited, but if they make a slight turn toward you, then go ahead and join the conversation.

Did You Catch That?

✓ Watching another person's lower extremities is just as important as watching the upper half of the body.

✓ Because the legs and feet are so far from the brain, people are not always aware of what they are doing with their legs and feet.

✓ The way you position your legs can tell people if you are open or closed to them and their ideas.

✓ How your feet and ankles point are a significant sign as to where you would prefer to be.

CHAPTER 6

Who Is Really in Charge?

The people in charge — the management team — and the ones who are regarded as being in charge are not always the same people. There is always the possibility that managers are not the most powerful people within the department or company. There are times when an employee has earned the respect of his or her fellow co-workers, and it could be because he or she is smart, honest, confident, or even bossy. This might give that person a false sense of being in charge of a situation or team of people, when, in all actuality, he or she is just like everyone else in the department.

Think about the nonverbal clues being sent by the people who lead us in our everyday lives, and how these people became leaders. There are some people who seem to exude the confidence and mannerisms of a leader, even as children playing on the playground. Then, there are those who learn it throughout their lives. A person may start out as a shy, timid, person who is unsure of who he or she is, but with age and good choices, his or her confidence and abilities grow. These people, along with the natural born leaders of our childhood, are some of the nation's top leaders in both business and government.

Natural-born leaders exhibit this ability even as children. When you were a kid and you were getting ready for a game of kickball, the captain of the team that you were on was probably the most confident kid on the team, and would assure you that your team was going to beat the other team. He was the kid that the whole team chose as captain because of his confidence and ability to lead. This was the same kid who, in high school, led the football team to win the state championship. He made you proud to be a part of the team or to sit in the stands knowing that he was your childhood friend and the leader of your team.

Through years of training and learning about their own body language and the language of others, naturally shy and timid people might have become leaders themselves in the workplace. Granted, it may have taken them longer to climb the corporate ladder than the already confident captain of the kickball team, but they made it with hard work and perseverance. They probably learned how body language works; fine-tuning their own to acquire the leadership stances that were inherent for others. They take their days in stride, and get jobs done well. You can read interviews with the top-earning moguls in this country, and some of them will tell you they learned and practiced confidence as they got older, because as children they were shy, kept to themselves, studied hard, and rarely attended school functions or parties.

Although every workplace has them, leaders are not the only people you interact with. This chapter will show you the different types of people you will encounter throughout your day. Remember that people can change roles within a company during their time of employment.

Influentials

These particular people display a sense of power. They do not have to hold a position of power, but they might have some powerful connections within the company. For example, the son of the top executive may be interning at the company in order to work his way up the ladder. He will automatically earn a great deal of respect because he is the son of the person in charge. This can be true for other employees who have a political connection or a connection outside the workplace. If a person proves that he or she has a connection outside the company with a political figure, such as the mayor of a town or the governor, then he or she might gain the respect of his or her peers more easily than someone who has no connection at all.

Being seen as an influential does not always mean that a person is given a powerful job title simply because of his or her connections. Sometimes, it is the personality and performance that earn a certain title. This is rightfully earned; it is not an inherited title. These people have gained the respect they deserve from working hard and being friendly to all levels of employees. Regardless of how a person becomes an influential in the workplace, the title carries certain nonverbal clues. People, in general, are more polite to those who have more respect, importance, or who are more powerful within the company. This is the common response, because these people are seen as the proverbial gatekeepers to others moving to a higher position within the company.

There are significant nonverbal clues that influential people use in the work environment that initiates an automatic response. These signals are typically things like sustained eye contact, firm handshakes, hands behind the back, and concealing their fingers (with only their thumbs being exposed). This position can convey both an uneasiness and confidence. A common response of people dealing with influentials is a friendly smile, lowered eyes, and constrained or closed body movements.

People are often seen as influentials because of the way they carry themselves — it is all about the attitude they portray. When they have the information another person wants or needs, they are seen as powerful. When the person with the information realizes he or she is needed, he or she has a tendency to show off a measure of confidence, displayed through body language.

Intermediaries

These people are known as the peacekeepers, and every office needs one. Intermediaries are good at defusing negative and potentially hazardous situations. These well-respected and valued people can work at any level in the company, although they usually earn respect for their tactful approaches to conflict. Everyone listens to them, especially when every other voice in the office is silenced, including the boss's. Because they are well-liked among the entire staff, intermediaries rarely feel the need to solicit a leadership role. They often advance automatically, without much of a challenge. Intermediaries will defuse any argument that may happen in the workplace. The typical signals of the intermediary are direct eye contact, firm handshakes, and casual body movements. Usually, people respond to them with friendly smiles, direct eye contact, and constrained body movements.

The intermediary can also take the two people having an issue with one another and sit them down to calmly talk about the situation at hand. For instance, Bill and Dave do not get along with each other for some unforeseen reason. The intermediary, Jane, decides she has had enough of the tension between the two of them, so she asks Bill and Dave if she can talk to each of them, acting as the intermediary. They both like Jane, so they agree to it. She asks them why they do not like each other. Bill, standing with his arms and legs crossed, tells Jane that he does not like Dave because he stole one of Bill's ideas and brought it to upper management, taking all of the credit for it. Jane then asks Dave, who was standing in the "fig leaf" position with a wide stance and his fist covering his genitalia, if this is true. During this conversation, both men are portraying strong, protective, and closed off body language. As Dave tells Jane that is not the case, his body language starts to shift. Dave told management that it was Bill's idea, but management would not give Bill the credit, because he was too intimidated to speak to them directly. Jane asks Bill how he feels about what was just said, and Bill says he does not appreciate being seen as a coward within the company. Jane then asks both men if there is a resolution to this issue that they can both live peacefully with. As the conversation carries on, Dave and Bill's body language changes from closed and guarded to more open toward each other. Once an agreement is made, there is peace between the two parties and they come to coexist in a workable, peaceful manner. Eventually all is forgiven and the two get along again, thanks, in part, to Jane, who never faltered from her open body language during the conversation as she acted as the intermediary.

Most intermediaries will remain levelheaded as they become more popular in this office role, but others might become arrogant. Even if the change in someone's leadership position is not official, the person's style and manner will change. Of course, his or her body language will change also, as the person begins to give off the signals of an influential. The body language of an intermediary will change from being open, to showing a new sense of power, with sustained eye contact, firm handshakes, and hidden hands.

Instigators

These types of people understand that others like to know more about other people in the office, and they use that knowledge to their advantage. They become masters at convincing people to tell them information. The instigator will in turn create trouble that only he or she knows how to control. He or she will often use what is known as the "back-channel," or the rumor mill, to get the information that he or she desires. The "back-channel" involves the lower-level members of the staff skipping over the official company ways of communication to anonymously share the information they have with senior level management. This will, in turn, create vulnerability in the levels that were skipped.

This person is known as the troublemaker. He or she will rule through intimidation or fear. He or she will probably be well received by some co-workers and loathed by others. The instigators are seen as powerful, though, because they have knowledge of new or relatively unknown information. If they are given this privileged information, then they might run an unofficial organization, or be able to dictate the climate of the work environment, which can possibly drive away good employees. Being able to read an instigator's body language should be a priority, because the signs of irritation could mean that there is trouble coming your way.

This person is essentially an actor, who pretends to sympathize with others, so his or her body language is always deliberate and calculating. Some people will be able to spot them easily, but others are unable to detect who the instigator is until he or she has put their career on the line. The instigator will probably have indirect eye contact and shifty eyes. The instigator will also often display protective body movements, such as crossed arms and an increase in personal space from the person dealing with him or her.

Intellects

These people are the brains of the business. They could have always been smart, or they could have simply mastered the job. These people have the respect of others, and people admire them because they are knowledgeable.

Although the co-workers respect them, the upper-level management positions might see them as a threat to their jobs. Sometimes, the responses they receive from others can vary. These people can be used by the influentials, and the instigators will probably have ill will toward them. The managers might feel threatened because not only do the intellects know how to do their own job, but know how to do every job in the company, or at least understand the basics of that job. This threatens managers because they feel that if one of the intellects has an idea that will benefit the company, and it is better than an idea the managers have come up with, the managers might lose their upper-level position to an intellect. The influentials, however, might will use intellects to their benefit by asking how they feel about a subject or an idea, and then use what the intellect said as their own idea, take credit for it, or use it to help generate their own ideas. The instigators might dislike intellects because of their ability to thwart the schemes the instigators have come up with. There are plenty of negative attitudes toward an intellect, as shown in the examples above, because of their ability to outsmart other staff members, and because of their ability to do everyone else's jobs. Many times, these intellects never receive the credit they deserve for the work they do. They know their abilities and will rely on those abilities to solve the problems and create avenues for themselves.

The body language signals intellects use are direct eye contact and open body movement. At work, people often respond to these types of people with narrowed eyes, furrowed brows, and protective body movements.

Insurgents

These people are malicious individuals who often threaten to sue, quit, or write letters. They are known as the troublemakers who rebel against organized standards because they are influenced by their ideals. They have the respect of others, but they will also be alienated due to a fear of retaliation. These people are often forced out or fired from the company, but some positive changes they fought to bring about may stay long after they are gone. They are known as a necessary evil in the workplace.

John liked working for his employer, but hated the standards he had to live by. He chose not to dress like everyone else in the company. Instead of wearing a standard suit and tie, he chose a more relaxed way of dressing, wearing a polo shirt and slacks. This was frowned upon according to company standards and he had been written up for it more than once. John decided to go to management over the dress code. He proposed, with a confident body language, that a relaxed way of dress would lead to a more productive day, and the only time that they would be in need of a full suit would be during a client meeting. He sat with his employer and maintained an open body language and listened to what he said and decided to try it for a week. After the week was over, the company saw a rise in productivity. They kept the new dress code. The other employees looked up to John because he held his ground when it came to dressing his own way. But, they also tried not to associate with him because they were afraid of being seen in the same light as John. They would avert their eyes when he was walking toward them or turn their bodies away from him, so he would not stop and talk to them. Although John's idea was ultimately accepted by his superiors, his defiance to the company resulted in his superiors asking him to resign, even though the way the office dressed remained the same long after he was gone.

The signals usually sent by the insurgents are a sideways glance, sustained direct eye contact, and lowered brows. They might dress in opposition to the standard and speak in elevated tones. The responses co-workers typically use are lowered or darting eyes, raised brows, and protective body movements and gestures.

Office Politics

Office politics exist everywhere, no matter how hard you try to avoid them. Your body language plays a major role in how your office politics work. The way it is sent and received will either prolong or shorten the process of how long the office politics take to play out. Body language can be a factor that adds fuel to the fire, or it can be a preventive measure in hearing the argument being had.

The employees who enjoy the political games in the office will use their body language to their advantage. They may not always be aware of their movements, but, without a doubt, most of them are using certain gestures on purpose. Some signs of people who play political games in the office are:

- Standing in front of the management, even though other employees tend to stand to the side or behind management

- Sitting as close as possible to the leaders of the group

- Acting important when the big decisions are being made

- Expressing their connections within the company

- Talking to all new employees to place themselves at an advantage

The employees who do not want to be involved in office politics will effectively use their body language, too. The difference is that their body language will usually convey an unpleasant or disapproving regard for the things going on. These gestures are used to avoid creating a scene, while still relaying the message that you do not want to get involved. Some non-verbal signs of disapproval of office politics are:

- Keeping your posture the same as you continue to do your job and not acknowledging the discussion, or distraction, as important.

- Treating everyone the same with open body language, such as a genuine smile, uncrossed arms and legs, and not gossiping about others.

- Keeping your focus on work with closed body language, such as keeping your legs and arms crossed, not turning toward the other person when he or she is approaching you, not turning toward the person spreading the gossip, and not trying to cause the distraction.

- Leaving the area where distractions or gossiping are taking place.

Sometimes office politics cannot be avoided and it can, and will, interfere with interactions at every level of business. Everyone has a co-worker who will step up the level of performance the minute an executive is within range, in an attempt to get that promotion he or she is so desperately after. These employees might try to curry favor with management, if necessary, to get the promotion. They may very well offer up their services for personal favors or even refuse to talk to the co-workers they feel are interfering with their chances of moving up in the company.

Keep in mind that in order to win the game of office politics, there has to be a loser. These losing battles can be in the context of isolation or a dismissal. If you were to be involved in office politics and be on the losing end, then your co-workers could end up keeping their distance from you, or you could be fired from your position. To keep from taking the brunt of the backlash, always try to perform above average.

Self-Assessment

Everyone receives feedback, to a certain extent, on the body language signals their bodies send out. It is important to self-assess how you are perceived, because it is easy to ignore the feedback or to be confused by what the feedback really means. If you observe your own body language in the workplace, you can make assessments and improve your own nonverbal behaviors, allowing you to make more effective statements in the future. There are typically four categories to pay attention to while doing a self-assessment:

- **Body position:** When you are speaking, is your body language saying you are confident and comfortable? Are you properly executing the correct body language position for the situation at hand? Are you coming off as interested and attentive to the needs of others? Are you positioning yourself toward the person that is speaking?

- **Facial expressions:** Are you expressing boredom, indifference, anger, interest, enthusiasm, or neutralization? Is it the correct expression for that particular situation? Are you giving off the correct response?

- **Eye contact:** Is your eye contact coming off as shifty or uncertain, due to how you limit it? Are you able to make the correct amount of eye contact with the other people in the room? Is it showing that you are neutral or confident? Is it held for long periods of time or is it direct?

- **Unconscious body movements:** Are you coming off as bored, impatient, or deceitful? Are you tapping your foot, shifting your weight back and forth, or drumming your fingers? Do you use frequent hand gestures, play with your hair, or shuffle the papers in front of you? What do you notice about your subconscious body movements?

How does she measure up? Her body language cues are saying that she is not focused completely on her work, or what her supervisor is saying.

Once you have finished this assessment, take note of the things you want to change and create a planned method for executing this change. If you are the type of person who likes to use his or her arms and hands quite a bit while making a point, then the next time you give a presentation, try to clasp your hands in front of you. The simplest way to control this type of subconscious body language movement is to first become aware that it exists, and then create a plan to stop it.

Repeat this assessment as often as you would like to gauge your improved body language. You can continue to make notes as you go along, allowing you to change other habits. This exercise can keep you aware and help you to effectively communicate your message to others.

Did You Catch That?

✓ There could be others who are, in some ways, more powerful than the manager.

✓ Find out who the intellects, insurgents, intermediaries, instigators, and the influential people are in the company, then make a connection with them in order to work successfully together.

✓ Those people who use their body language to their advantage are often the ones who play the game of office politics.

✓ Body position, facial expressions, eye contact, and subconscious body movements are the four categories to use for a self-assessment — use them to improve communication through your body language.

CHAPTER 7

Interacting with Various Audiences in the Workplace

Body language plays an important role in verbal communication. You could be selling, negotiating, supervising, researching, meeting, or listening, and what your nonverbal clues say to the other person is of the utmost importance. Corporate climate, job turnover, and morale are all affected by how well verbal and nonverbal clues are communicated. Companies should offer to train their employees in effective interpersonal communication methods, because communication is just as important as hiring a competent staff to help your business go to the next level.

Body language is different for every level of command in a business. Though an executive will always use an official form of communication, including print media, reports, memos, or pamphlets, to relay an important message to all staff, an entry-level employee might use e-mail or even a phone call to relay the same message. Every person in a company has his or her own style of relaying messages to other staff members. Understanding and adjusting your own style is crucial to building better communication relationships, because it will allow others to receive your message more easily.

Research states that every individual differs in the sending and receiving of signals to and from one another using the four communications styles —

closed (passive), blind (aggressive), hidden (passive-aggressive), and open (assertive). Discovering what type of communicator you are is important. This will help you determine how effective you are in the office. If you use one style of communication, it is important that you vary your ways to incorporate a little bit of each of these styles, thus optimizing your communication skills in the workplace.

Shannon, Mark, David, and Jacob all worked for the same company and worked in close proximity to one another. There were many times they would be assigned to the same projects and had to communicate with each other to get the projects done efficiently. Typically a closed communicator, Shannon never had much to say, and rarely sought out feedback from her fellow co-workers. Her passive way of communicating, however, always got the job done well, and most of the time, she would not even make eye contact with the three men she had to work with every day.

Mark, on the other hand, gave everyone he talked to too much information, including information about his personal life; however, he did not expect, or want, his co-workers to share their own thoughts about their projects. He would express his talent for the business, but in the process, he would be very demanding and criticize everything else that the rest of the team worked on. Mark is what is known as a blind, or aggressive, communicator, because he would always state his opinion and be demanding, but could effectively complete the job he was assigned.

David was the most well liked of the foursome. He would never divulge too much information, but he always wanted feedback on the information he gave. He would listen to everything anyone said to him, but he was known as a "yes" person and would just go along with what the group wanted, instead of putting his own ideas on the table. David is what is known as a hidden, or passive aggressive, communicator. David would never state his own opinion — he would just agree with whatever everyone else in the group said, even if he knew the ideas would not work. But, once he was assigned a task, he would incorporate everyone's ideas to get the job done effectively.

Jacob was an open communicator. He not only gave out the information and feedback needed, but he also expected the rest of the team to do the same with him. He treated everyone as an equal, and showed everyone the same level of respect. When Jacob presented an idea, he would ask the team their thoughts. Once he was given feedback, he would tell them what he thought about what they had said. During this time he always kept his body language confident and open, which made for a calm discussion with all the members.

A big project was coming up, and this foursome was elected to do it. Jacob proposed an idea to get the job done faster, but with the same result as if they worked "by the book." David, being the "yes man," immediately agreed to this plan. Mark, on the other hand, did not think it would work. Shannon, when asked her opinion, disagreed with Jacob and thought they should stick to the way the project was initially supposed to be done. Jacob listened to her reasoning, and then told her that if they did it his way, it would save the company money and time. After an hour of everyone going back and forth over how the project should be done, an agreement was reached. The final decision was they would stick to the book as much as possible, but would integrate Jacob's idea to get the job done in a time-efficient manner. Having worked together so much, they knew the appropriate way to communicate with each other, and the project was able to get done in a timely manner while saving the company money.

Knowing what signals to look for when it comes to every communication style is important when you are working in close proximity with people every day. This will help you be a better communicator and make your day easier, with fewer confrontations and the ability to resolve any conflicts that do arise with greater ease.

You can tell when someone is a closed communicator, because he or she will not give you much communication and will hardly seek feedback. Like Shannon, a *closed communicator* will usually be more comfortable working with objects rather than with people, and is usually passive in nature. These types of communicators will go by the book when making a decision. Here are typical behaviors of closed communicators:

- **Eye movement** – Their eyes will be lowered or darting. They will have infrequent gazes.

- **Facial expressions** – They will raise their eyebrows.

- **Body movement** – Their body language will be closed off and restricted. They will have a limp handshake and their head will be tilted.

- **Style of dress** – They will have a more conservative style of dress, mostly in neutral colors.

This employee's crossed arms and condensed stance are the first hint that she is a closed communicator. By touching her neck and avoiding eye contact, she might be trying to remove herself from the situation.

The *blind communicators* will share too much information, but will not ask for feedback and will usually take a covert, aggressive approach to communication. These types of people, like Mark, prefer to show off their knowledge and skills. They often demand things and criticize everything. Blind communicators will tell you to do things for them, while giving you all the information you need, and some will criticize everything you just did for them in return, even if you followed their instructions. Although their actions may be aggressive and overt, their communication is blind in the sense that they are not open to receiving communication from others. Here are typical behaviors of blind communicators:

With a blind communicator, sometimes the verbal and nonverbal messages are mixed, because the cues do not directly match up. In this picture, the positioning of the employee's hand on her hip and her clenched fist reveal tension or aggression, while her sustained eye contact indicates her concentration.

- **Eye movement** – This type of personality will sustain direct eye contact with piercing eyes.

- **Facial expressions** – They will have lowered eyebrows.

- **Body movement** – Their hands will be expressive. When they shake your hand they will use the glove or two-handed handshake to convey their dominance. Other hand gestures will let you know their mood or personality.

- **Style of dress** – They will usually wear high-end, natural fabrics with designer labels.

The *hidden communicators* hardly ever give out information, but they will want feedback. They are typically known as the good listeners and are liked by most everyone, just as David was in the earlier example. Some hidden communicators, however, are the passive-aggressive type, who might seek revenge or manipulation. They are usually called the people pleasers and known as the "yes" people. These types of people will be in agreement with everything that is said in a meeting, even if it is not the best choice for the company.

Here are some typical behaviors of hidden communicators:

With one arm crossed and a shifting eye and head, this employee is using hidden communication to convey neutrality, even if that is not her true sentiment.

- **Eye movement** – They will not make direct eye contact and may have shifting eyes.

- **Facial expressions** – They will have one eyebrow raised during the conversation and they are quick to smile.

- **Body movement** – They have a closed or restricted body language. Their hands will touch some part of their face during the conversation.

- **Style of dress** – They will usually dress in brand-name clothes of a neutral color.

The *open communicators* will give out information and want feedback. This can make some people uncomfortable, depending on how personal the communication gets. Open communicators, like Jacob, will show respect and appreciate others while still maintaining an assertive personality. This can possibly be the best way to do business, but in situations where conversations need to be simple and quick, this is not usually the best way to conduct business. Although giving and asking for feedback on their performance and ideas can be a good thing, sometimes a meeting with the interviewer, boss, or client is on a timeline, and the conversation needs to be kept within that time limit. Therefore, there is not always a chance for the open communicators to receive the type of feedback they seek. Here are some typical behaviors of open communicators:

- **Eye contact** – They will usually sustain direct eye contact.

- **Facial expressions** – They will raise their eyebrows and give a big, toothy smile.

- **Body movement** – Their body language will convey openness and they will give a firm handshake upon meeting you.

- **Style of dress** – They will have a casual and relaxed style to their clothing.

With a relaxed but upright posture, this employee is keeping her body language open from head to toe to appear approachable.

Customers and Potential Clients

Business is all about the way you communicate, even from the first few seconds of a phone call. Your receptionist's upbeat way of answering the phone can land you a potential client — the person on the other end of the phone should be able to tell if the receptionist is smiling simply by the tone of his or her voice. If the tone is upbeat, and the receptionist is perceived to be smiling, the client will assume that the business fosters a friendly but professional work environment. Likewise, when your customer enters into your office, the body language of your fellow employees will leave an impression long after the customer has left. Open and friendly gestures, such as smiling and eye contact, show respect and openness to the customer, making him or her more likely to return to the venue.

There are some businesses that will not have a desk or chair for their employees, therefore decreasing the distance between the employee and the customer. There are some banks with a self-service area, where the customer service representatives are waiting nearby in case you are in need of assistance. There are some banks that will send someone to assist you while you are waiting in line so as to provide faster service. Cell phone stores will have their employees approach the patrons instead of having them come to a desk for service. This type of behavior can be seen one of two ways by a customer. Depending on how the worker acts, it can be viewed by the customer as pushy or aggressive, or the customer might see it as helpful and caring for his or her needs. This all depends on how the approach was made. If the customer service representative displays a closed body language or comes toward the customer in a hurry, then the customer likely will view them as pushy or aggressive. But, if the customer service representative comes toward the customer with open body language, such as keeping his or her arms at his or her sides, using a genuine smile, and placing the palms of his or her hands toward the customer, then the representative will be seen as being helpful.

There are unique challenges when it comes to customers and clients. The employee must quickly figure out the customer's communication style and find a way to approach him or her to see what service the person is in need of. Regardless of your work environment, whether it is an office or a store, being able to tell a client's communication style just by observing him or her is important, especially when it comes to closing a deal. You can do this by:

- Asking the client as many questions as you can and really listening to his or her answers. This will help in your quest to find out how the person likes to communicate his or her needs. To show the client that you are really listening to what he or she is saying, you must be facing the client at all times, mirroring his or her body language, and giving nods at the appropriate moments.

- Researching the client's past professional and personal history, when appropriate. This will give you an idea of how to deal with this customer. Based on your client's past, you will be able to see how he or she may have been persuaded to invest in other companies. You can use this information to your advantage, as you are able to remain confident and portray an open body language so the client knows you are open to listening to his or her needs.

- When you are dealing with a client from another country, researching which gestures are seen as an insult in the client's culture is a key element. *For more information about how culture relates to body language, see Chapter 12.*

- Consider the person's gender and age. A person's age can cause his or her body language to be slower, and whether the person is male or female causes a difference in the reading and sending of body language cues. *For more information about how age relates to body language, see Chapter 12.*

- Being more formal and showing more respect in your body language is the most important factor when trying to seal a new relationship or make a sale with a potential client or customer. Be open, but be passive to a certain extent.

Being more formal means keeping your body language to a minimum; act like you are in an office setting and be professional. Having an open body language is good, but avoid being too relaxed, like you would be around your friends. Being too relaxed will come across as unprofessional, and might make your client feel as though his or her business is trivial to your company. Thus, it is important to pay attention to your own body language, too, especially when speaking with a new client face-to-face for the first time.

Remember to:

- Keep your facial expressions pleasant and have a relaxed, yet confident, body posture.

- Place yourself at a 90 degree angle from the client so you do not seem confrontational. Instead, you will portray that you are trying to tell the client something that no one else may know, making him or her feel more important, whereas sitting across from him or her makes it seem like you want to keep your distance and might not understand his or her needs.

- Maintain the proper amount of eye contact — 15 seconds of eye contact at a time is recommended; anything more makes the person feel like you are trying to intimidate him or her, and anything less makes you seem shady.

- Avoid fidgeting during the conversation so you do not give off the wrong body language cue of being disinterested or nervous.

- Keep an eye out for body language signals that tell you if the client is bored, irritated, or that you have entered his or her personal space.

Appropriate body language for your clients and customers

When dealing with a client over the phone, you can take advantage of the fact that he or she cannot see you. But, because they cannot see you, you have to rely on your voice for communication strategies — your tone and pitch have to relay the message that body language cues usually do. For example, standing up, instead of sitting down, makes your voice sound more powerful and authoritative. You must keep your focus on the phone call, so avoid fidgeting or surfing the Internet because then you will be distracted, and the client or customer will be able to hear it in your voice.

Focus on an object as though it was the customer or client, and maintain "eye contact" with it. The customer will hear the concentration in your voice and will know that you value him or her. Some nonverbal gestures, however, should still be used even when your client cannot see you. For instance, smiling on the phone is necessary because, even though the person on the other end cannot see your smile, they will be able to hear it in your voice. When you smile, the pitch in your voice typically differs from when you have a straight face. The pitch will rise slightly, but it will rise enough to be noticed by the person on the other end. This, in turn, makes the person on the other end of the phone feel like the company is a good place to work, and that will probably make him or her think more closely about using the company for his or her needs.

Depending on the type of work you do, sales or customer service, your body language cues will differ. Customer service representatives will look to maintain a business relationship, whereas salespeople will use their body language to gain a new relationship with a potential client. The customer service representative will learn the basic body language cues to make the customer feel like the company values him or her. The salesperson, on the other hand, will learn a variety of gestures and methods to get the client to use the product or service.

A customer service representative is either securing a new client or helping one that is already a part of the business, so he or she might just use the same type of body language as the rest of his or her co-workers. The customer service representative will typically use open body language to appeal to the potential customer with agreeing gestures, such as a nod, as to avoid being pushy or aggressive toward the customer. The salesperson, on the other hand, will not know what type of person he or she will be in contact with, so it is essential to know how to appeal to every type of person. Salespeople need to be wary of how their nonverbal cues are coming off, to ensure they do not turn off their potential clients. Standing too close or touching the potential client too soon can be seen as an aggressive way of communicating, which can potentially blow the chances of making the sale. It is also crucial for salespeople to make customers feel respected and valued, just as customer service representatives do, by mirroring the customers' language, and showing them open, confident body language when speaking about your products and services.

When formal business negotiations are taking place, every element can make a big difference, even if it seems as trivial as where you sit. Where and who you sit next to can send a message to the other people involved. For example, the power position is usually at the head of the table, so if you want to be seen as a powerful member of the company, then sitting near the head of the table will benefit you. A reassuring message can be sent by sitting to the side of the customer, and not directly in front of them. Some things to avoid so you do not seem intimidating to your potential customer or client are a challenging stare, large gestures, and keeping your posture in an upright position. You want to avoid being too aggressive or too submissive, because it will turn the client away from your company, sending the client in the direction of your competitors.

In order to make the most of your business meeting with a client, try implementing, and avoiding, the nonverbal cues from these lists:

Nonverbal cues to use with customers and potential clients

Nonverbal Cue	Typical Meaning
Maintaining eye contact and looking up in consideration	You are listening to what they have to say and are giving thought to their points
Extending and exposing your palms	You are open to what they are saying
Standing with your feet slightly apart	You are not tense or trying to rush
Nodding or slightly tilting your head	You are compassionate or are trying to understand what they are saying
Smiling	You are being cordial

Nonverbal cues to avoid with customers and potential clients

Nonverbal Cue	Typical Meaning
Shifting or darting your eyes	You are not paying attention
Putting you hands near your face or touching your face	You are not comfortable being there with them
Fidgeting with an object, such as a necklace, hair, or pen	You are not paying attention to what they have to say, and you are anxious to have the conversation end
Placing your hands on your hips or behind your back	You are hiding something or are not being honest with them, or you have a problem with what the other person is saying
Standing with your arms and legs crossed	You are closing yourself off and are not open to what they have to say
Locking your fingers together	You have closed your mind off to anything they have to say

If the potential client or customer comes off as a closed person, then ask certain questions to make him or her more open to your ideas, products, and services. If you were able to research the client before hand and found that the person is generally a closed customer, preparing a presentation to address all the concerns he or she might have is the key to getting the customer to accept your ideas and services over your competitors' proposals.

The most educated customers you will have are the blind communicators. Before ever having a face-to-face meeting with you, these customers will research you, your product, your service, and your competitors. These types of customers know more about what they want than the average customer; therefore, how you communicate with them is of the utmost importance. Showing off your knowledge and confidence about your product or service is important to keep these potential clients or customers. You should keep your posture upright, make the appropriate amount of eye contact, smile, and give a firm handshake when entering and leaving the meeting to show your confidence.

The hidden customer will want the product or service you offer to be well-known and reliable, so be prepared to provide this type of customer with names or numbers of people who are able to provide testimonials about the quality of your product or service.

Perhaps the easiest customer is the open customer, who will tell you what he or she wants or needs. These customers will require a more personable interaction, involving touching and smiling. They will want you to show them information about the product that can be verified easily. Open customers want things that they can easily verify, because they want to ensure that they are getting the most for the money they are about to spend. Using confident body language during the meeting makes it easy for the client to see that you know what you are talking about, making the information you are telling them easy to verify. If the customer or client does not like how the information is being relayed to him or her, or cannot verify the information, the customer's body language will start to turn to the closed type of body language, showing that he or she is losing interest in the sale. If the person is expecting a high return on investment and can see that he or she will be getting his or her money's worth, the customer will then display open body language.

Interactions with Employees, Managers, Executives, and Colleagues

Supervisors and managers use their personalities to effectively balance their authority by delegating tasks to get projects completed. The managers who think communication with their employees is a closed path — those who expect employees to listen to them, but do not listen to their employees — are ineffective at getting projects done. However, managers who keep the lines of communication open, by listening to their employees, are often successful in getting things done. To be successful and effective managers, their body language needs to be open and their verbal clues need to match. Being receptive to an employee's feedback will help make the company a success, but it can only be done by understanding the various styles of nonverbal communication.

Appropriate body language for your co-workers and managers

Keeping an open style of body language while your employees are telling you how they feel is important. Even if you do not like what you are hearing and want to close off, try to keep your body language open and receptive. Likewise, employees should always pay attention to the verbal and nonverbal habits of their managers and colleagues. Once you are able to determine the style of management, and the communication habits of your colleagues and supervisors, then you are able to figure out what is expected of you throughout your workday.

Closed employees usually will want to have a conversation only about the task at hand. They want to get the job done, and not be involved in the personal aspects of a business relationship. They will not require much verbal or nonverbal interaction with their fellow employees or management team. Their animation and nonverbal responses are limited during the conversation. Some managers will be less direct and have limited interactions with their employees, giving them little supervision. The self-motivated and self-directed individual will work well with these types of managers. In the same respect, the colleague who is closed will not have much interaction with fellow co-workers. These colleagues will not give much of a response verbally or nonverbally, and they often work well on individual projects.

Employees who use a blind communication style tend to just want the basic information when given a task. They will want to show you what they can do with their skills and knowledge, and will often take a defensive stance if you try to show them a more efficient way of doing their job. When it comes to speaking, they will ignore all the nonverbal signals of the person they are trying to communicate with, because they do not want your feedback; they likely want to tell you all the information they can. Therefore, these managers are blind in their communication, but if they feel that they have been overlooked, they will openly express their disappointment. They will have an aggressive body language when approaching a group of employees or individual who has made a mistake. This is an attribute of the blind communicator ,because he or she has a tendency to be more aggressive than passive, passive-aggressive, or assertive. These people want things done — done now, and done right the first time — but they will expect you to know this without ever expressing their expectations.

Suggestions on how to improve a process or possibly contributing ideas while completing a task is an attribute of a hidden employee. This is considered hidden because these types of communicators are passive and will usually want your opinion on everything they do, so they will ask what you think of the ideas they are contributing. These employees need plenty of affirmation and reassurance, because they are very sensitive to closed or hostile forms of body language. These types of people are generally shy and will avoid a person who has a hostile or closed off attitude. They will not make much eye contact throughout a conversation, if any is made at all. They will get the job done, but prefer to work on their own. They will listen to what needs to be done, but will not respond unless they are asked to. Managers who are hidden communicators are also known to be deceptive. His or her smile will be faked, or forced; he or she may bite the inside of his or her mouth; or he or she may shove his or her hands in his or her pockets. This type of manager might not convey much information, but the information he or she wants will be for his or her own benefit.

Although most employees, such as hidden and closed, prefer to work alone, open employees work better in a group. They can be overly friendly when speaking with management about making improvements and other issues but are the best at taking criticism. The managers who exhibit an open communication style will appreciate an employee's openness and honesty about business affairs. These types of managers are willing to hear and share personal affairs with other open employees, especially if it will affect productivity at work in a positive way. However, they might have clothing and body language that is too casual for the workplace environment at times and might not show up to work in a suit, but rather in a polo shirt and slacks. He or she is trying to appeal to the employees with a friendly attitude. Generally, the friendly attitude of an open communicator makes these managers and colleagues well liked by the other employees, because they come off as the more understanding of the communicators. Plus, with an open communicator, colleagues are always aware of where they stand with their work and relationships in the workplace.

Ultimately, managers need to understand how each employee communicates, and how that style affects his or her ability to get the job done. Although each type of employee communicates in a different way throughout the workday, there are certain nonverbal cues that should be used, or avoided, by everyone.

Nonverbal cues to avoid when dealing with employees, colleagues, managers, and executives

Nonverbal Cue	Typical Meaning
Rolling, shifting, or narrowing your eyes	You do not believe what they are saying
Furrowing your eyebrows	You are angry or do not believe what is being said
Lowering your head	You are disappointed or insecure
Sitting with your hands behind your head	You think you are superior to your employees
Crossing your arms or legs	You are closed off to what they have to say

Rubbing your head or neck	You are unsure about what they are suggesting
Tapping your foot while they are speaking to you	You are impatient and want the conversation to end
Rocking back and forth and fidgeting	You are no longer paying attention and are distracted
Pointing your finger or pounding your fist	You are angry
Lowering or darting your eyes	You are avoiding the speaker or not paying attention
Clapping your hands slowly	You are being sarcastic

Nonverbal cues to use when dealing with employees, colleagues, managers, and executives

Nonverbal Cue	Typical Meaning
Keeping direct eye contact with them	You are listening to what they are saying, or you are confident
Keeping your hands at your sides or in front with your palms exposed	You are open to what they are suggesting
Standing with one foot slightly forward	You are not tense or intimidated
Nodding your head during conversation	You are compassionate; you are listening to what they are conveying; or you agree
Smiling	You are being cordial
Sitting upright	You are alert
Only gesturing with your hands when explaining a choice between options	You are exhibiting self control
Smiling less than they do	You are showing that you are professional

Did You Catch That?

✓ There are four basic types of communication styles used by everyone in the workplace: closed, blind, hidden, and open.

✓ In order to appropriately approach a customer, the worker must quickly determine the communication style of that person to decide what nonverbal cues will be most effective.

✓ The manager should always be open and receptive to employees' feedback and should demonstrate this through his or her body language.

✓ The employee can better anticipate what the manager expects by understanding the style of his or her communication.

CHAPTER 8

Unlearning Behavior Patterns

Competence and ability can earn you success in the workplace, but sometimes you need more than just that — managers and executives usually notice an employee's attitude just as much as his or her ability. The people who complain about the job or other employees are known to have a negative attitude and are often disliked by the management team. This person might be labeled "the boy (or girl) who cried wolf;" meaning, his or her complaints are often unwarranted and are usually ignored after a while. Even when this person has a justified complaint, it might be overlooked because everyone around them has become desensitized to the person's complaining. These people might be overlooked for promotions, even if they are competent employees. Then, there are the employees who rarely say anything, but perform satisfactorily on the job. They, too, are usually overlooked for promotions.

It is the assertive, or confident, employees who garner attention from their employers, even if their performance is less satisfactory. They tend to ask questions before confronting anyone about anything that has been done or said. They will be respectful when expressing their feelings or opinions on various subjects in the workplace. Their body language consists of a confident behavior, without being overly cocky.

Everyone has learned how to respond to different situations either from parenting, socialization, or perhaps a little bit of both. You tend to go with the behavior pattern that makes you most comfortable, even if you do not respond to a situation in the same way every time. This is referred to as your personality or disposition. There are major fields of research about this because of the world's fascination with behavioral patterns. The professions of psychology, sociology, marketing, and gambling are all based on being able to determine predictable behavior patterns within another person or group of people.

It's more than just bluffing

When people are playing a card game against one another they have to be able to read the other people at the table in order to see if they are bluffing, or if they actually have good hands. For instance, in a poker tournament, in order to be able to reach the final table you often have to win at least ten tables. To do this you must be able to read the body language of the other players. You will see the players pull out all the stops, so that their opponents will not be able to read their body language. Some players might wear iPods to calm themselves; others will wear sunglasses, so their eyes are not expressive. Some poker-playing champions, such as Phil "The Unabomber" Laak, will even go so far as to wear a hooded sweatshirt with sunglasses, tying up the hood around his face after making a large bet so other players cannot see his expressions. Then, there are the poker players who do absolutely nothing to cover their body language or expressions, such as Phil Ivey. He has learned to control his actions so the other players cannot tell if he is bluffing or if he has a good hand. He will sit there stone-faced, never moving a muscle except to fold his hand or move chips into the pot, all the while ignoring other players who are trying to intimidate him. When some players have a good hand, they will shift in their chairs and move around. When they have gone all in, putting all their money in the pot, they will stand up and walk around due to nerves. Ivey does not do any of this; he stays seated without saying a word, using behavior patterns that other players have failed to learn in order to further his own winnings. It has worked — he is one of the most successful professional players out there, because he was able to figure out what kind of communicator he is, and use that to better his career.

Overcoming negative behaviors

Determining what type of communicator you are can help you to overcome a negative behavioral pattern. People will always be able to tell someone what he or she wants to hear, but their body language might tell another story. How a person might greet you can tell you about the mood of that person, or even his or her personality. How your receptionist greets your client or customer as he or she enters your office can play a pivotal role in whether or not he or she will continue to do business with your company. Clients or customers are able to pick up on whether the receptionist likes or dislikes his or her job, or whether he or she is having a good or bad day. Thus, it is imperative to unlearn behaviors that convey a negative attitude.

Facial expressions and some other factors, such as body language, play a pivotal role in detecting a person's disposition and possibly his or her negative attitude. Juries are forced to make snap judgments when it comes to a defendant who chooses not to testify. The jurors will probably watch a defendant's facial expressions throughout the trial to determine the accused's feelings about what was said throughout the trial. In order to determine what to say or how to behave toward a customer, salespeople will "size up" a customer by paying attention to his or her body language cues. The salesperson is able to tell whether that customer wants to be approached, what he or she might be looking for, and the disposition of the customer. If the salesperson reads the cues wrong, he or she may drive the customer away by using his or her own body language to send the wrong message. The salesperson must learn to keep his or her body language open in order to convey to the customer that he or she is understanding of his or her needs.

When someone is labeled with having an attitude, it generally means that person has a bad attitude. The body language of the person with the attitude is often negatively displayed. Sometimes, the person who has the attitude never knows that he or she is labeled this way, because this is how he or she has always carried him or herself. This person could have learned it from his or her parents or the environment he or she grew up in. Two of the most detectable dispositions are aggression and arrogance. These two dispositions use very clear gestures and facial expressions. People need to give off the appropriate nonverbal messages in order to be effective in the business world, because there are ideas, often stereotypes, made about a person at first glance. You do not want to give off the wrong impression.

Determining your personality

Do you come off as passive, aggressive, pessimistic, optimistic, or assertive? How can you tell how others see you? Identifying different reactions in the workplace will help you understand variations in your colleagues' responses to the same situations. This is not to say that certain personality types are ineffective in the workplace. Most individuals can be placed into several categories rather than just one. Try to determine which of the following descriptions match your personality and figure out which ones are the complete opposite of you. Understanding all of these personality traits will help you to communicate with your colleagues better. If you do not know the difference in personalities, then, much like the salesperson, you might send the wrong message with your own body language to your colleagues. Learning all the traits of these personalities will help you unlearn the wrong body language cues that you might send in response to the other person.

Depending on your genetic make up, socialization, and conditioning, you can be any one of these types of people. Some gestures are natural, such as a smile. Blind people smile, although they have never seen someone do it. How you cross you arms can be due to your genetics, too. One way will feel comfortable, but the other way will not. The environment you grew up in can have an effect on how you carry yourself. If you grew up in an environment where you were constantly teased, you probably have developed either a passive or an aggressive attitude. If you grew up in this type of environment, you might be timid or shy and have more closed body language, or you might have become defensive and your body language will be that of an aggressive nature. Your parents condition you to think and act certain ways, but those ways are not always acceptable. The longer you are around someone, the more you are apt to pick up some of his or her personality traits. If you are sharing an office space with people who are constantly complaining and carrying themselves with negative body language, you might start to do the same thing. If you are talking to someone who sways while he or she talks, then you will probably start to do the same thing during an extended conversation. If any or all of these behaviors are a part of your personality, you will need to unlearn these types of behavior in order to be more successful in your career choice.

If you have a more aggressive behavioral pattern, perhaps due to childhood trauma, then becoming passive aggressive will enable you to become more successful. Instead of charging up to a co-worker, try to walk calmly and listen to his or her side of the situation before forming your conclusions, or succumbing to anger. If you are the type of person who complains, then try to find something positive about your day, and focus on that. This will help you to unlearn the negative behavior associated with complaining. It will open up your body language more, and you will become happier than you normally are. If you are generally a negative or an aggressive person, seek out a person that is more positive and open in the office and try to spend more time with him or her. You will notice yourself changing and taking on some of his or her personality traits; this will help you to overcome the negative behavior associated with you. The following scenarios are designed to help you determine which type of body language habits you use, and which ones you need to change.

Let It Go — Passivity

A manager of a sales company sets up a lunch meeting to discuss the new system for tracking sales data. She has discussed everything about the new system and is hoping to end the meeting at the scheduled time. During the meeting, her body language remained open and she was pleased by how the meeting was progressing. A colleague, however, has a many questions about the new system, so the meeting continues for another hour. Another colleague offers to help with any questions this person has after the meeting has concluded. But, the rest of the colleagues decide that it is an open forum and begin expressing their concerns about the new system. The manager continues to answer questions, but she is hoping that her employees will realize that she is annoyed. During the last portion of this meeting, her body language turns to being closed. She started to bite her nails while listening to the questions and even fidgets with her pen while answered the questions in hopes that the room will notice her behavior and end the meeting. She crosses her arms and legs, but continues on until all the questions are asked and answered.

This manager is acting passively. This is the type of person who backs off or completely walks away from any form of conflict. Passive people can be less effective in business because they have trouble solving problems by always giving in to other people. This behavior pattern might cause other employees to overlook them, especially the ones with an aggressive nature. With this behavior pattern, there is a need not to disappoint or offend other employees. They tend to take on too much work in order to please others and often will fail at completing those tasks. They may be considered willing team members, but they are often not brought onto a team because they can be unreliable.

The passive behavior usually begins when people are afraid of others not liking them or having to be "yes" men in order for their fellow colleagues to like them. This passive person is also known to be a closed communicator. There is usually low confidence level with people who have passive personalities, because to them, other people's views or opinions are more valuable than their own. People with dominant positions are often threatening to those who are passive. This is because passive people do not always believe they have a right to express their views or ideas. Their fear of rejection is what holds them back, and they do not know how to become more powerful. All of these attributes can be shown by the following signals:

- Avoiding eye contact

- Hunched shoulders

- Burying hands in their pockets

- Biting their nails

- Fidgeting or fiddling with things during a conversation

- Crossing one arm across their chest

- Stammering or stuttering

Some passive people feel like they do not have a right to express their opinions, which might make them appear nervous or uninterested in the situation at hand.

What Did You Say to Me? — Aggression

The manager of a business wanted to make sure that all of his employees arrived on time to work every day, so he implemented a policy that required every person to stop by the receptionist's desk so she could record what time everyone arrived each morning. One employee arrived five to ten minutes late every morning, because she had to drop off her son at day care across town. She would make up the time and stay late after the office cleared out, and she was even more productive after hours than she was during the workday. Once the manager heard about her late arrivals, he confronted her about it. He walked over to her desk, shut off her computer screen, and proceeded to tell her that if she was late one more time, she would no longer have a job. She suggested altering her schedule so that she stayed late in the evening to make up the time she was late each morning. He yelled at her, asking why she thought she had the right to question his authority. He proceeded to pound his fist on her desk and lean near her face after she questioned him. His reaction to her suggestion, and how he handled the situation overall, is an example of an aggressive disposition.

These types of people can be ineffective in a business setting, because they tend to dwell on the problems they are having and might ignore a reasonable solution in favor of winning an argument. This type of behavior may alienate other employees and cause a breakdown in the communication process. A passive person, on the other hand, will typically submit to this personality type or otherwise avoid dealing with them. At the cost of respect or of maintaining a professional relationship, aggressive people will often get what they are after because of the way their confrontational body language intimidates others. These nonverbal body language cues will alert you to a potentially aggressive person in the workplace:

- Unblinking stare

- Narrowing eyes

- Pursing their lips as if to hold back what they are saying

- Tilting or jutting their chins

- Pointing their fingers in an accusing manner

- Clenching their fists

- Standing with hands on their hips

- Invading your personal space

- Striking a nearby object

- Clasping hands behind their back

- Talking loudly in order to dominate the conversation

- A high-pitched, fast rate of speech

- Making others wait intentionally

Aggressive personality types often instigate confrontation and are easily irritated.

No Way, Not Happening! — Negativity

A colleague sits in a meeting, listening to the details about franchising the company. With the franchise comes more paperwork and more assignments for everyone, with the possibility of working longer hours. She does not see how doing more work will benefit the employees, but everyone else seems to like the idea of the franchise. She believes the company did not plan this well enough and is sure it will fail. She thinks the decision will not do the company any good and that it is based solely on greed, so she stops listening. She shifts from an open body language in the beginning of the meeting to closed body language in the middle. She crosses her arms and avoids eye contact. When she is asked about her opinion, she shakes her head back and forth. She does not want to comment on the situation until another employee encourages her to do so, almost forcing her to speak. She keeps her body language closed, even while she gives her opinion to express her irritation on the subject. She states that she does not feel this idea is going to work and she cannot understand why the management is not happy with what they already have. She is an example of a negative disposition.

Negative personalities do not believe they can easily handle a problem. They can be ineffective in a business setting because they will often ignore the possible positive outcomes, or they might ignore the potential of the company, much like the employee in the above scenario. They often do not see the positive in a situation and usually are opposed to change. For example, they might think a new, creative idea is not good and might oppose optimistic views about expanding their business. They are avoided by most of the other employees because of their negative demeanor. They usually like delivering bad news, so they are often the ones who gossip about office happenings. This behavior comes about because of a hopeless feeling about their own situation.

Negative personalities feel defeated and will often project this feeling onto others with these nonverbal signals:

- Closing their eyes when spoken to or wandering eye movements

- Rolling their eyes in disbelief of what someone is saying

- Looking down or away from the person speaking to them

- Crossing their arms and legs

- Pinching the bridge of their nose in disgust

- Shaking their heads in disagreement

- Resting their hand or finger on their cheek

Crossing their arms and looking away are key signals of a negative attitude. With this closed body language, this employee is not interested in communicating.

Why Bother? It Won't Change Anything — Cynicism

A decorated ten-year veteran of a company was told his office was now being moved to a shared space on the first floor of the building, and that a recent college graduate was moving into his office. He was given no reason as to why this change was being made, but a fellow employee told him that the company needed the space due to an expansion. She said that most of the company's employees were being shifted around, and the college students were going to get all the nice offices. He argued that he should have been one of those few employees allowed to stay in his office because of his loyalty to the company. She suggested that he say something to the upper management, and he said he would not even bother because it would never change the outcome. He thought about the other times when he was overlooked by the company's management, and he thought this was an unfair move by the company. While this conversation was happening, he became defensive. He locked his ankles, crossed his arms, and kept his chin down. He is an example of a cynical personality.

The cynics are the ones who believe no one has been able to take care of a problem. These people are usually ineffective in a business environment because they regularly complain about the problems they are having. They often are not interested in a solution to a problem — they just want to complain about the workload. They show disdain for the environment in which they work. They limit the potential of other employees because others see them as less effective. Negative employees are different from cynics — cynics will provide hard evidence and reasons for disagreeing with the speaker, whereas negative employees will disagree without being able to provide a viable reason or evidence. They often compare people and bring up past events in order to make a point about why they think something is unfair. Cynics often show their personalities with these types of body gestures:

- Roaming eyes when speaking

- Moving their eyes from side to side when listening

- Raising their eyebrows while listening

- Pointing chins down during conversation

- Crossing their arms and legs

- Locking their ankles

- Rigid handshakes

Combined with her crossed arms, the facial expressions of this employee convey her cynical personality.

I Know What to Expect and What Is Expected from Me — Realist

Some colleagues at a company worked on a presentation for months for their fellow engineers at an upcoming convention. One of them created most of the material, while the other organized and designed the project. Their system was very effective — when one person finished the research on a topic, the information was given to the other member for design. Two days before the presentation, the computer malfunctioned and the designer lost all of the work he had done.

There were two choices. The first one was to call their boss and postpone their presentation to the last day of the convention, which could give them ample time to get the computer to the repair shop so they could recover the entire file. It might be costly, but they knew their colleagues would appreciate a full and proper presentation. But, regardless of how technologically savvy the repair shop was, there was a possibility the file could not be recovered. The second choice they had was to give the presentation at their scheduled time. They could retrieve the last file that was sent by e-mail and work from there. This presentation would only be halfway done, but they would not be disappointing their boss and fellow colleagues with a delay.

One of them wanted to pursue the first solution, no matter how much it cost, even though there was the possibility that the file would not be able to be retrieved. The other preferred the second solution, because she felt the first solution meant taking an unnecessary risk by wasting time and money. She is an example of a realist. The first person slumped in his chair, as if giving up, and rubbed his face with his hands. The second person remained calm and poised.

The realistic people of the world will tell you just what type of trouble lies ahead. They might have a tendency to be ineffective in the workplace, however, because they often will not consider more than one solution to a problem. They prefer a hard solution that is sure to work to an easy solution that might not work. They typically use absolute words, including "must," "only," "never," "always," and "perfect." People tend to conform to their ways because they are less threatening than the other personality types — a realist will take the points of all parties into consideration, but then he or she will express his or her opinion in a matter that allows everyone to understand and agree upon the decision. Their body language allows people to be more relaxed around them. They often believe that they hold the standard for truth due to their straightforwardness. They avoid risky ventures because they stand by their practicality. They can be mistaken for pessimists, because they avoid taking risks.

There are times when a realist will peer over his or her glasses, as if to say, "Give me a break." Although this might just be a way of conveying a realistic approach to a problem, it can be seen as condescending. Realists also tend to touch their face while listening to a co-worker.

Realists, however, will take calculated risks, whereas the pessimist will not take any risks at all. If things do not go as expected, they will make decisions that will provide some form of security. The body language of a pessimist and a realist differ. For instance, a realist might peer over his or her glasses at the optimists or pessimists to convey that he or she is considering the ideas being discussed. Sometimes realists can be seen as condescending, but you will know that this is not the case when, in combination with peering over his or her glasses, you see the person form a small steeple position with the hands. Additionally, his or her legs will stay in a parallel position, or he or she will stroke his or her face while you convey your ideas to him or her. Usually, people who are realists use these types of nonverbal cues:

- Maintaining direct eye contact
- Peering over the top of their glasses
- Forming a steeple pose with their hands
- Keeping their legs in the parallel position
- Stroking their face during conversation

Anything Is Possible — Optimism

Sophie was a relatively shy person in meetings who would rarely speak her mind, so before the meetings, her manager, Bill, would come to her and ask for her opinions. She would then tell him what she thought should be done. Bill would, in turn, take her ideas to upper-level management. Eventually, someone went to the management team after a meeting and told them that it was Sophie who had given Bill a particular idea earlier on. The management team approached Sophie and asked her why she would let Bill take the credit. She said did not mind it too much, because it was for the greater good of the company. Sophie took an optimistic view, acknowledging the fact that her ideas were being used for the company's benefit, even though she did not initially get credit for them.

The optimistic people are the ones who believe that any problem can be taken care of if they try hard enough. They might be ineffective in the workplace, because they fail to plan adequately for bigger obstacles. The optimist will only see the positive outcome of things, and might not plan for all the obstacles that may appear. They are known to focus mainly on the solutions to the problems that lie ahead, so they are typically well liked by everyone except the negative and pessimistic employees, who criticize them. Pessimists dislike optimists because of their ability to see the positive in everything, whereas the pessimists only see the negative. They are seen as the ones who think things are better than they truly are and that everything will work out for the best. Optimists generally use the following body language cues to convey their hopeful attitude:

- A wide-eyed stare
- Rubbing or clasping their hands
- Exposing their palms
- Having an erect posture
- Walking briskly
- Talking in a high-pitched tone and at a fast pace

Everything about this employee portrays her optimism, from her large gestures to her erect posture and her big smile.

I Can and I Will — Assertiveness

A manager wanted to stop his employees from using a conference room for their leisure time. There were items stolen from this room, so no one was allowed to enter it without written permission. He noticed that today one of his employees was in the room working on the budget. He reminded this employee that using the room without permission was in violation of the company policy, and he could be written up for it. The employee informed him that he is constantly interrupted and distracted at his desk, which is why he was in the room in the first place. By taking it upon himself to work in the conference room, regardless of the manager's policy, he acted in an assertive manner.

Assertive personality types will confront a problem head-on and deal with the outcome, whatever it may be. They can be the most effective people in a business, because they will analyze a problem from every side. They will tell you what they want to happen but will usually ask the necessary questions and listen to all the responses given. They have an understanding of other people's feelings, because they often take the time to listen to what is being said, and in return, other employees listen to them. They will request something from someone instead of demanding it, but they will actively disagree when they see fit. They have the respect of most of the employees, but passive people will see them as aggressive because they state their feelings, thoughts, and desires. The confidence and mutual respect between them and their co-workers can be shown through these body gestures:

- Maintaining direct eye contact

- Having erect posture

- Displaying the arms in an open position

- Exposing the palms

- Keeping their legs parallel

- Giving nods to show comprehension

- Talking in a moderate pitch

This employee is ready to confront any problem the workday brings. Her assertive personality is shown with her erect posture, solid eye contact, open and relaxed arms, and nearly parallel legs.

Unlearning Behaviors

To avoid experiencing the effects of a rough economy or competitive industry, overcoming ineffective behavior patterns is crucial. Identifying how others see you, which could be as one or a combination of the behavioral patterns described in this chapter, can be the biggest step to changing your nonverbal cues. When people get to know each other, they learn to expect certain responses and actions. Behavior is generally more noticeable when it is different or uncharacteristic of a person. These behavioral changes inform the other person as to when something has gone wrong or when something is unusual for that person.

When people learn what patterns need to be changed, they tend to conform to the opposite of that pattern, attempting to move away from the negativity associated with their initial habit. The first changes can be extreme. Think about an aggressive person resorting to a passive behavior pattern and the opposite happening, where a passive person turns to aggressive patterns of behavior. These behaviors will change again to be more moderate when they receive and accept the verbal and nonverbal cues from their peers. Either of these behaviors can be received well or received badly, depending on the colleagues of that person. When a person is known to be passive and then suddenly feels the need to become aggressive, it can be a shock to some, yet well received by others. His or her body language will go from being closed, with the arms and legs crossed, to being more aggressive, with nonverbal cues like a "charging" walk toward the other person, finger-pointing, and a scowl on his or her face.

For instance, Sophie, the optimist from the previous example, is generally a shy person and she keeps to herself, even when going out with her girlfriends. While she is at work one day, she gets fed up with being taken advantage of by her manager. He is taking her ideas and passing them off as his own. She decides to confront him about it. She marches into his office and starts yelling at him for taking her latest idea for his own. She stares at him, points her finger at him, and even invades his personal space. Taken aback by her behavior, he suddenly becomes like a child being scolded by a parent and does not know what to say to her. In the following days, every time he walks past her he ducks his head, and when he has to talk to her he avoids making eye contact with her, and suddenly has a stuttering problem.

The entire office is proud of her for standing up for herself, but they are also concerned about the manager because he has become completely passive. This may not have been the most effective way to unlearn her passive behavior, but for her, it was a success. The other employees saw this as an even more negative behavior pattern than her optimism, especially when they were approaching her to ask her a question. When she realized what was going on, she apologized to her co-workers and said that she would try to be less abrasive. The happy medium was simply asserting herself. She was able to tone down the aggressiveness and not be passive at the same time. Her co-workers listened to her ideas and implemented them, giving her full credit.

Walter also learned to change his behavioral patterns in the workplace. Usually, Walter is a cynical man who does not think that saying anything will help the issues he is having in the office. Instead, he complains to himself, or to another trusted employee, Carol. He was complaining about a problem he was having with the new budget and how he felt it would not work. Carol told him that he should tell management how he felt about it. His response was the same as always — there is no point; it will not change anything. Carol still encouraged him to try. He took her advice and went to management about the budget. He showed them confidence and mutual respect by using direct eye contact, speaking with a moderate pitch, and giving understanding nods when he was listening to their side of the conversation. When he came back from the meeting, he told Carol how he was able to get management to come to an understanding. She was proud of Walter for being assertive, but the next morning in the daily meeting when Walter asserted his opinion on another matter, not everyone was as receptive. John, a pessimist, saw everything as being a bad idea. He went to Walter and expressed his feeling while shaking his head and crossing his arms. Walter remained confident and told John why he decided to use an assertive style of communication. After listening to Walter's reasons, John's arms uncrossed, and his hands formed the steeple position. John had changed his way of thinking from pessimism, because he recognized Walter's point.

Did any of those scenarios sound familiar? Do you remember using similar body language cues? These scenarios can help you figure out what personality type you are, as you can take a step back and see yourself as others see you. Then, you can change the negative connotations of your behavior with some practice. It can be hard to unlearn your behavior pattern, because you have become accustomed to that pattern, but it is doable. The more you practice, the faster you are able to unlearn your bad behavior.

Did You Catch That?

✓ The best way to unlearn behaviors is to come up with a plan for eliminating negative body language.

✓ The two types of immediately detectable personality traits are aggression and arrogance because of the involvement of obvious gestures and facial expressions.

✓ Seeing yourself as others do can be the biggest step in changing your behavioral patterns.

CHAPTER 9

Nine Scenarios in the Workplace

It is the first interview with a possible manager or your first time bonding with new colleagues — these are just a few common workplace experiences, and your body language is an important factor in each one. Being too relaxed in an interview, finding it hard to relate to other employees, or receiving negative reviews from your managers despite your performance can all be signs of how people respond to your body language. As you have discovered throughout this book, your body language can speak volumes about you. The impact of these messages is often most easily recognized in the reactions of co-workers. Showing confidence in yourself and your abilities to do the job from the start will propel your career.

Because the body language you display at work strongly hinges on your reactions to the events that happen throughout the day, your gestures are always giving off a certain vibe to your co-workers, employees, or superiors. This chapter will walk you through nine different scenarios that you may face at work — starting with your first interview. This way, you can get a glimpse of how to make your body language work for you.

1. Interview with a Manager

When you are invited to a second interview, it can be more stressful than the first. The first interview could be a phone interview, which only required you to be professional over the phone, enabling you to wear whatever you wanted. You could conduct last-minute research about the company during the interview, and you could even stay in bed. The second interview, however, will require you to actually go to the office to meet with the person that could be your new boss. You want to appear confident, which means dressing to impress in business attire appropriate for the position. You want to be able to say all the right things and answer the questions that you are asked, but you also want your body language to convey that you are the person for the job.

Within seconds of meeting a potential employee, a manager has made an initial impression. Starting an interview with a positive tone and open, confident body language will help make a good impression that will last far after the interview.

Within the first five minutes, employers usually know whether or not you are the person they will give the job to. Not only are dress and appearance important, but other nonverbal cues are just as important. Everything combines in those first few minutes to give your employer a lasting first impression. To ensure you give off the "hire-me" vibe, try using these nonverbal cues:

- **Describe yourself in a positive manner.** When you do so, make sure you use erect body language to show confidence.

- **Describe your past with positive personal stories.** Smile while speaking about the past events to convey positivity.

- **Express opinions that are in agreement with the Interviewer.** When agreeing with the interviewer, nod your head at the appropriate times.

- **Claim responsibility for successful events at other jobs.** Make sure you have an upright posture to show that you are proud of your accomplishments.

- **Compliment the interviewer or the company.** Smile and raise your eyebrows to show your interest and how impressed you are while telling him or her how much you like the company.

- **Tell the truth.** If you try to embellish, your facial expressions and body language will change. There are companies that will have the same people conduct all interviews, and they will be able to read your body language. These people will be able to tell by your movements whether you have told them a lie, or whether you have told them the truth.

- **Only use your hands for gesturing.** The only gestures you need to make with your hands are the ones that will add meaning to what you are saying. Make sure that your palms are exposed throughout the interview so that you give off an air of openness and sincerity. Do not touch your face, hair, or mouth. You might want to leave your hands resting in your lap and separated comfortably.

Using appropriate and modest hand gestures can help emphasize a point, but be sure to keep them controlled.

Although some hand gestures are useful to help demonstrate your point to the interviewer, avoid using large hand gestures during an interview.

- **Leave the interview with confidence.** Always give direct eye contact, smile, and firmly shake hands with the interviewer upon leaving. Even if there is a group interview, you should still follow the same protocol.

When interviewing for any position, you must remember to have a proper balance of both control and enthusiasm. Use the following tips to help keep your body language, and you, on track:

- **Sitting stiffly throughout an interview is never a good idea.** Sitting completely still throughout the interview might disturb the interviewer. Shifting periodically is OK as long as it is not too extreme.

- **Smile less than the person conducting the interview.** Big smiles and giggles throughout the interview make you appear goofy, silly, or unprofessional. This speaks volumes to the interviewer on how you would present yourself to the executives of the company and it could be interpreted as a cover-up for your nervous energy.

Having too big of a smile during an interview can make you appear overeager or unprofessional. Mirror the body language and smile of the person who is interviewing you so your personalities do not clash.

- **Not smiling at all is not the best idea, either.** You are not expected to have a straight face throughout your interview. When presenting yourself in a positive light, smile. If the interviewer is telling you about an amusing situation in the office, it is OK to smile. If you do not smile, you might be seen as cold, and you may not be hired because your potential employer will feel that you will not be a good addition to the office.

- **Make eye contact.** Showing respect and being truthful are important during an interview, and making eye contact while you speak will help you achieve this. If you are asked a question and respond with a "yes," but look away when saying so, then the interviewer will know that you are being untruthful with them.

- **Do not stare down the interviewer.** Too much eye contact can seem like you are trying to intimidate the person into giving you the job. You are allowed to look away or look at another part of the person's face for a brief moment.

The most remembered attributes of a job candidate are facial expressions, appearance, and eye contact. The final impression can make or break your chance of landing the job. If you come into the interview in a negative light, you have the potential of leaving the interview in a more positive light with the right body language and facial expressions.

2. First Day on the Job

The first day on the job is always a bit stressful. You are unsure of where you will sit and if you will get along with your co-workers or managers. As you hope for enough work to fill the day, you try to portray yourself in a positive light, attempting to win over the rest of the staff. There are ways to show you are competent and confident when starting a new job, all of which deal with how your body language will be received by your new colleagues:

- **When arriving for your first day, be on time and show some enthusiasm for the position.** Getting a full night's sleep will give you the energy you need to meet your fellow colleagues and you will be able to keep pace with the activities of the day instead of having sluggish body movements and gestures that indicate that your are disinterested in your job. You will be able to walk in to the new job with a genuine smile on your face, instead of a forced one, which you might have if you are groggy.

- **Always dress professionally.** A person in a business suit is seen as a competent person. This will also help you maintain your confidence level and keep any nervous body language to a minimum. The better you dress, the more confident you will feel, which will be reflected in your body language. When you are seen by others as being confident, you will act confidently.

- **Make a great first impression.** It takes a mere four seconds for someone to make a first impression. People will begin to judge you when you are two feet away from them and by the very first sentence you speak. You must present the best possible you — remember that everything you say and do, how you dress, how you breathe, and how you hold yourself will be under scrutiny on your very first day.

- **Give colleagues your undivided attention.** Not everyone is going to send you a good vibe, but it is important to still pay them the same courtesies you would anyone else. By the end of the day you might be exhausted from shaking everyone's hands and listening to stories about the person who held your position before you, but it is important that you still show the same smile and give the same firm handshake all day.

Your first day after your promotion

Being promoted within the same company can be more stressful than coming in from a different company. Maintaining the friendships you had made can be more stressful, too. There can be an air of resentment from your friends if they do not feel you deserved the promotion. There might be a lack of respect, because they still see you as a peer and will refuse to take orders from you. Use these tips for showing off your competence in your new role:

- **Do not compromise your new position for anyone, but remain friendly.** As you make your way up the corporate ladder, there will be those who get left behind. There will be some who are jealous, resentful, or even disappointed. There will be questions about your trustworthiness from people you considered friends, because you have become a part of the management team. You can still have a friendly conversation, but do not tell them confidential information just to prove that you have not changed. You should keep your body language the same as you did when you were the same rank as them — it should be open, friendly, and full of confidence. If you need to be authoritative, you need to have confident body language that does not waver when others complain.

- **Don't sweat the small stuff.** Becoming overly emotional about the hard time you might receive after taking a step up the corporate ladder shows that you lack self-control. Keeping your body language positive, with an upright posture and a smile on your face, will keep you poised and in control of your emotions.

- **Always remain firm in your decisions.** If you say one thing with confident body language, then do not change it or allow it to be more casual to satisfy your friends. Casual body language that changes to more of a slumping position will result in a lack of respect.

- **Make sure that you act the part.** Shuffling your feet while walking, slumping in your chair while on a conference call, or spilling food on yourself during lunch might

Remember that the way you dress directly reflects on your attitude for your job, and the clothes you wear greatly influence your body language. The way you dress can also influence the way others see you, especially after a promotion. This outfit would not fit in with the dress code of most workplaces.

have been overlooked by your peers, but now that you have been promoted, these acts are seen differently. And, these things are probably not seen in a positive light by other managers. You must dress and act the part in order to be successful in this new role.

3. Meeting a New Client

Landing a new client is one of the most important aspects of a salesperson's job. From your appearance to your manner of speaking, everything can affect the way a client or customer responds to you, and just one slip-up can cost you the deal. Your body language should always remain open when you are trying to land a new client and build a rapport with them. There are a series of gestures you can use as a way to exhibit open body language:

- **Mimicking your client's body language.** When two people talk for a period of time, they tend to mimic each other's body language. This is a way of showing the other person you are trying to be on the same wavelength as him or her. It can be seen in a positive light from the person you are trying to build rapport with. When the client leans back, then so should you. When the client crosses his or her arms, so should you. This will let the client know you understand what he or she is saying.

- **Relax a little.** Keeping a relaxed demeanor helps to put your client at ease. If you are warm and friendly and you treat your client as an equal, you can build a better rapport, and might even land the account. Keeping your arms at your sides with your hands visible at all times is highly recommended, unless it is a lunch or dinner meeting and you are eating. There is a consensus of trust when a person's hands are visible during a meeting, because it signals that the person has nothing to hide.

- **Pay attention to your seating positions.** If you are meeting a potential client at a meal or in another business setting, always take the seat that is facing the other people in the restaurant or business area. This way, your client will only be facing you and he or she will not be distracted. If you are sitting at a table with four corners, make sure to sit on the side that is dominant to the client — if he or she is left handed, then sit to the left to ensure direct eye contact.

Gender plays a role in how people like to be seated. Two women will sit in a booth on opposite sides and will still be able to have an important conversation. Two men, on the other hand, will sit a small table at right angles so they can have an important conversation. A man and a woman will sit opposite each other at a small table, so the same private conversation can be had as the other two. When having a private conversation, women will speak in hushed tones and have a tendency to slightly lean over the table, whereas men will not lean toward each other. The man and woman will lean toward each other, on the other hand. These seating positions happen for a reason. Typically, the two women sit this way out of comfort, the two men find common ground within the 90 degree angle, and the man and woman feel reassured by sitting across from each other. With all of these seating positions, you will be seen as non-confrontational, making the dynamic between you and the other person more comfortable.

If your first meeting with a client is at a restaurant, it is crucial that you remain in a calm position while you wait for your server to arrive. By rocking side to side, touching your face or hair, and crossing and uncrossing your legs, you appear unprofessional or insecure — giving bad signs to the client you are trying to woo.

The man and woman in this photo were able to find common ground with their seating positions, because the angle between them eliminates a power struggle. With erect posture and an almost expressionless face, her body language is not mimicking his directly, and could make him uncomfortable in this situation.

- **Be wary of the distance you keep.** You might get closer to people than they prefer depending on your culture or the type of person you are. You need to be aware of just how close you to your client, as to not make him or her uncomfortable while you are speaking. Intimate and casual spaces are the two major components of keeping an adequate distance.

Your intimate space is from 0 to 18 inches around your body. When you are this close to a person, you will be able to get a sense of the person's fragrance and see every square inch of his or her face. Your casual, or personal, space is anywhere from 19 inches to 4 feet from your body. This amount of distance will allow you to speak in a conversational tone and read the other person's body language; something you cannot do if you are standing directly on top of somebody. Any distance further than 4 feet will make it hard for you to keep the attention of the person you are speaking with. It is advised to start at a distance of 4 feet, and move closer as you both become more comfortable with each other, but be careful not to get too close.

Be aware of the other person's body language — if you start to move closer and the person moves away, recoils, or shifts uncomfortably, the person is not approving of the decreasing distance and it is best that you remain where you started.

- **Listen and speak in a conversational tone.** The client you are meeting with has done his or her research on your company, so trying to sell yourself, or your product or service, is not necessary. It is important that you listen to your client's needs and then propose a plan that will suit those needs. Keep your tone of voice casual and conversational so as not to try to dominate the conversation or intimidate your client. Mirroring the client's body language, or keeping your body language open as the client speaks shows them you are listening to what they are saying to you.

- **Give your undivided attention.** This is a sign of respect for the client. If you are respectful, the client can build a rapport with you, increasing your chances of landing a new account. When you are giving your undivided attention to a client, make sure to nod and smile at appropriate times, as well as lean forward a little while speaking and make appropriate eye contact.

When you are meeting with a new client, it is important that he or she knows that the only thing important in that moment is your ability to meet his or her needs. Using the preceding tips can help you land a new client for your company.

While discussing ideas, it is important to keep your body language open to reflect your frame of mind. In this picture, the forward lean shows interest in the content, while hand gestures and pointing show that the co-workers are engaged.

4. Brainstorming Meeting

A company meeting often falls into two categories: great or terrible. Depending on the people attending the meeting, the task being explored, and the end result of the meeting, meetings can often lean more toward the terrible side. A conference that has very involved participants, on the other hand, might make for a great meeting. These meetings involve co-workers who come up with a plan of action that includes dates for the completion of tasks and deals with all the pertinent issues before the meeting is over with. These are productive meetings. People talking over one another and not arriving at a consensus can force meetings to end with resentment and headaches, making the meeting inefficient.

Throughout a brainstorming meeting, all participants contribute their ideas and work collaboratively to form an outline for solving the problem at hand. You could be leading or acting as a contributor to the meeting, but your great ideas might never be heard over the shouting that can occur unless you use the appropriate body language to accompany your thoughts.

- **Sit in a prime location.** Your position at the table can draw the attention of the other participants. If you happen to be the one leading the meeting, then sitting at the head of the table is ideal, but if this seat is unavailable, position yourself under the wall clock — employees are sure to look in this direction to keep their eyes on the time. You can also position yourself by the door, to the direct left or right, or in the center of the long table; these are all primary positions. While you are in the prime position, remember to keep your posture upright, not to fidget with anything, and to hold your hands at the midway point with your palms exposed. All of these body language cues will convey that you are listening and willing to participate in the meeting.

During a meeting or presentation, placing one hand to your chin will let others know that you are actively listening to the speaker and processing the information.

- **Let people know you are deep in thought.** You should show the room that you have been thinking about the topic at length through your body language cues. Some of these cues are cradling your chin while looking to the right and allowing your hands to form the steeple position. The steeple position of your hands shows people you are thinking about what is being said, or that you are contemplating your next move. Cradling your chin also shows that you are deep in thought, or makes it seem as though you have much on your mind. The people in the room will notice that you have been thinking about what is being said and will want to hear what you say when it is your opportunity to speak.

- **Lean forward while addressing the room.** If you are leaning forward, it makes you look like you have something important to say. You may notice that the other people around the table will lean forward, mimicking your body language. People commonly sit in this position when they are trying to hear what someone is whispering. It is guaranteed that if you lean forward while speaking, people will pay close attention to what you have to say.

- **Appeal to your audience.** Use a variety of hand gestures will help you communicate with your audience and get them to agree to your point of view without even realizing that they do. What is commonly known as the fish gesture, holding both hands apart to indicate the size of something while keeping them in line with each other, conveys the idea that you wish to project your thoughts into your audience's minds. When you move your hands from your chest to point at your audience still holding this gesture, it conveys that you are projecting something to them. If you hold your hands out and spread your fingers, you are hoping to connect with the entire room. This gesture is showing the audience that you are pointing at them all, as if you are including each of them in the conversation. If you are standing with your palms facing upward, then you are making a plea to the audience for their support. You will see this when the presentation reaches a point where affirmation is needed from the audience. If you are using your palms to push downward, you are telling the room that you would like for them to settle down. When a debate gets heated, or the audience is just settling in, the speaker will use this gesture to quiet the crowd down so the meeting can continue.

Each gesture is universal and can help you to connect to your audience better by making them feel like they are a part of the conversation. By doing this, you can make a better connection and get a better response from your audience. If your presentation is about selling your product or idea to a company, then making them feel like they are a part of the conversation helps you sell your product or idea to your audience.

Using the fish gesture during a meeting or presentation can help you sink your point into your colleagues' minds. This gesture is often used to show the size or importance of something.

5. Bonding with New Colleagues

It is in human nature to want to form immediate bonds with colleagues at the beginning of a new position. After a few weeks of work and attending meetings, you might automatically be included in their circle of friends. However, if the friendships are not easily made, you will have to make more of an effort, especially with your body language, to get your co-workers to open up with you.

When you are attempting to become friends with your co-workers, you will need to listen to what they are saying, as well as read what their body language is telling you, in order to determine what their personality might be. By talking with your colleagues, you can tell which ones are sociable, who has to be the center of attention, and who is a proverbial wallflower. The sociable people will have an open body language and smile at you as you enter their space. The person who always has to be the center of attention will interrupt a conversation when uninvited. This person will, often times, have a slumped posture with a frown on his or her face in hopes of someone asking what is wrong. The wallflowers will not make much eye contact, because these people try to keep to themselves as much as possible.

Regardless of what type of personality someone has, there are many reasons why people choose to act the way they do. If you take a quiet co-worker to a small café, he or she might become more comfortable with you than if you took the same shy co-worker to a noisy sports bar. When you have figured out what type of personality the person you are bonding with has, you can attempt to bond with him or her by complimenting his or her personality and communication style. There are many personality types that you will encounter in the workplace, which can make communication even harder. Some of these office personalities were discussed in Chapter 7, but you can use the following list to help you understand six of the most basic personalities:

- **Manipulators** — These individuals typically want to gain as much control over a situation as they can. They will use sweeping arm gestures, firm handshakes, and cross their arms over their body, all in an effort to get their way.

- **Experts** — These people often believe that they know everything. They will either stare or avoid the eyes of others in an attempt to hide if they are lying. If the person is avoiding eye contact, it might mean the person is unsure of what he or she is saying.

- **Reactors** — This type of personality will react to the emotions rather than the facts of the situation. They will shake their heads often and blink rapidly, because they are reacting to the things they are hearing, or they are nervous. They will be in disbelief of what they hear, causing them to fidget and have a slumped posture.

- **Complainers** — These people will like nothing better than to have you listen to their problems and sympathize with them. They will use angry, open, and pleading hand gestures to convey their message with urgency and disbelief.

- **Pleasers** — These personality types might conform to other people's ways of thinking, just to be liked by everyone in the office. There will be much smiling and head nodding from these people. They want to fit in with the rest of the office and will sometimes do anything to accomplish this. They will mirror the body language of who they are speaking to in attempts to build rapport with that person.

- **Pricklies** — These personality types appear abrasive on the outside, but they likely are just protecting their sensitive nature on the inside. They prefer a great deal of distance between themselves and others; they are fast walkers, have a downward gaze, and they cross their arms.

Usually, once you have figured out what type of personality someone has, you decide whether you want to get to know this person better. It is up to you whether you want to form a closer bond with this individual after you have discovered the person's motives, personality, and reputation. If you want to become closer with this person, there are a number of ways you may do this in the work setting:

- **Agree or respectfully introduce another point of view.** You might not agree with other people's point of view, but stating your own in a harsh manner, with closed, aggressive body language, will not be the way to win friendship. If you do not agree with them, respond by receiving what they are saying with open body language. If you want to interject your own opinion, then an affirming nod and tilt of your head to the right shows them that you are interested in what they have to say. If you are in agreement with this person, then be sure to nod and smile.

- **Decrease the space between yourself and your co-workers.** Sitting closer to them or leaning in when you speak will let them know you are trying to bond with them. If they do not jump backwards or flinch, it is a sign that they are comfortable with you doing this. If they move closer to you, then they trust you.

- **Accept invitations.** If you are indeed bonding with them, you will be invited to do something after work. If you are new to the company and trying to gain the respect of others, this can be one of the biggest milestones to overcome. When you are bonding with your co-workers, you should maintain open body language or build a rapport with them by mirroring their body language.

- **Avoid negativity.** Of course, there are the possibilities of unwanted advances, meeting someone that turns you off, or finding out about a person's negative reputation. It is best to then keep your distance from this person.

Taking the time to bond with your employees, colleagues, or employers is important, because it can ease the mood of the workplace. With a little effort on your part, you will be able to open their body language so they are accepting of you in your new position.

The main thing to keep in mind when trying to bond with your co-workers is that your body language is key to overcoming any situation — even negative ones. For example, Steven was the type of person who really wanted to be a friend to everyone. He was kind and well liked by many people, but when starting a new job he always found it difficult to make new friends right away. He was starting at a new company on Monday and had decided he would get to know everybody as quickly as possible to be accepted into the inner circles of the workplace. He had been there a week and had made some nice connections with everyone. He was talking with Natalie when he noticed Mike, Natalie's jealous ex-boyfriend, coming toward them from the corner of his eye. Steven had already decided he was not going to be friends with Mike because his body language, which was always closed with a scowl or frown, made him seem like he was mad about something. Steven could not understand how someone could be like that at all times, but as Mike approached, Steven decided to diffuse this situation before it got worse, so he asked Mike how he was doing, with an open body language and a smile on his face. This seemed to calm Mike down a bit, and he joined in the conversation about the day's workload with a calmer demeanor than he usually had. Because Steven used his body language to correct a potentially problematic situation, he was able to build camaraderie with Mike and his other co-workers.

6. Respectfully Declining Further Contact with Others

There is always one person in an office that everyone tries to avoid for a certain reason. Maybe this person is an instigator, the office gossip, or just has a poor attitude. Because most of your waking hours are spent at the office, you want to avoid those people who make your life more difficult than it has to be. Sometimes this is easier said than done, especially if this person is your manager. There are always ways that you can avoid these personality types in a respectful way. There are three types of individuals you may want to avoid: clients, colleagues, and managers.

Clients

Clients might keep you in business, but they can be demanding with your time, leaving you unable to assist your other clients' needs. The demanding client will call you day and night, claiming everything is an emergency so you will respond to him or her in a matter of minutes. This person is never satisfied. You can go without answering the phone call, or putting all of this client's e-mails in a folder for review later on, but when he or she shows up at the office, it becomes a problem. Use these tips to handle this sticky situation with your body language alone:

- **Take control of the impromptu meeting.** When the client makes a surprise visit, you have to meet him or her, but make sure to enforce a strict time limit to hear what he or she has to say and address any concerns. Nodding your head in affirmation will make your client feel as though you are listening, and make him or her feel like you are concerned about the problem. At the end of the time limit, summarize what the client had to say, firmly shake hands, and show him or her to the door.

- **Meet in an open area, possibly with uncomfortable seating.** The client is less likely to be loud if you are in an open area. If your client wants a meeting room or a closed door, you might say it is not possible because the meeting rooms are all occupied and your office is too small for two chairs. Sit or stand close to the client and talk in a hushed tone of voice. This will tell the client that this will not become a screaming match. The purpose of sitting in uncomfortable seats or standing is to make the client less cozy than he or she would be in your office, thus speeding up the process of the meeting. You will start to shift and so will the client.

- **Politely stress that this visit is not warranted in the future.** Always show your client courtesy, but make sure he or she knows in the future such a meeting will not be accommodated. Blocking a doorway or crossing your leg across your body lets the client know you are restricting access to the office. This will give the impression that your client is not welcome to come to the office without a scheduled meeting.

Colleagues

There are colleagues who will want to talk your ear off all day, instead of doing their work. These colleagues get little or no work done but will know everything that is going on with the company. Some people would rather work and find these people distracting. Use these tips to respectfully end your role in the office chatter or gossip:

- **Avoid making eye contact.** Avoiding the person who comes over to chat while you are really busy is often not as hard as it seems. Do not make eye contact or even look in his or her direction. If you do not give your colleague your undivided attention, he or she will probably understand the hint and walk away from you. When the person starts a conversation, look at your pile of work to indicate you are busy and simply cannot talk.

- **Ask your colleague to repeat his or her words.** If the employee you are avoiding is the office gossip, then ask him or her to repeat what was just said. If the gossip is trying to tell you about someone, it will be done in a hushed tone. Ask him or her to repeat the words, but more loudly this time. Your colleague will respond to this by telling you that he or she will come back later. If your message got across, your colleague will not return to your desk for the rest of the day.

- **Make sure you are unavailable.** Walk at a fast pace when you see them in the hallway, lunchroom, or copy room. A quick smile and a head nod as you walk past them will let them know that you are acknowledging their presence, but you are not available to talk to them.

Trying to dodge a chatty co-worker can be difficult, especially if you feel cornered. Hold your ground by keeping closed body language — avoid eye contact, close your legs, and lean back in your chair to create distance between you.

7. Marking Your Territory Without Speaking

Being in an open space affords you the luxury of backing away from someone who steps a little too close to you, but when you are in a cubicle, it is impossible to back away from someone; because the space is already limited.

Jay was sitting in his cubicle working when the office gossip, Laura, appeared at his desk. As much as he wanted to ignore her, she always made it impossible because no matter how hard he tried to avoid her, she would still ramble on. She would always want to lean in and talk to him so no one else would hear the conversation. He would try to deter her from doing so, but he should have tried to create distance between himself and Laura so she might not have been so persistent on sharing the office gossip.

Here are tips for placing some distance between you and the other person in a corporate setting:

- **Lean back in your chair and cross your legs.** Do this when someone is approaching you while you are in your cubicle. This pushes your upper body backward and your lower body forward, allowing you to occupy more space than you would while sitting in an upright position. If you stretch out your body to make it look longer than it is, it will give you more space and should send the message to your co-worker to move backwards.

- **Cross your legs inward.** Crossing your legs so one foot points inward will deter people from breaking into your space while you are talking to others in a group or in a one-on-one situation. If you are sitting with your foot pointing outward, it tells the person you are not completely engrossed in the conversation. But, if you are sitting facing the other person and your foot is pointing inward, the person will be less likely to interrupt the conversation you are having.

- **Close off your body language.** When you are having a conversation that you do not want to be having, cross your arms. This will signal the other person that you are closed off and are not paying full attention to what he or she has to say.

The easiest way to portray that you are not listening to your colleagues, whether during a meeting or a one-on-one conversation, is to close off your body language. As shown above, the crossed arms and wandering eyes show a disinterest in what the other person is saying.

- **Standing up during conversation.** If you are short on time and unable to have a long conversation with a colleague who likes to talk, stand up when the person starts speaking. Moving around your cubicle gives the impression that you are getting ready to leave for a meeting. Doing this helps you get that person to understand that you are short on time, and he or she will either keep the conversation short or wait until he or she has more time to talk to you.

8. Showing Confidence When Communicating with Your Manager

After being in a new position for a few weeks, you might begin to see the real personality of your manager. When there is stress or pressure, people will act differently. Some managers can become impatient when they are normally very attentive to the needs of their employees. Some might become visibly angry when the pressure is too much — you will see them clenching their fists or their veins pulsing on their foreheads. Then there are those who release their anger in a verbal manner. With these types of managers, you need to know how to use your nonverbal cues to express your confidence:

- **The Tyrant** – These types of managers treat you as if you are a child and they are your parental figure. They probably will not give you the opportunity to make your own competent decision, nor will they tell you that you are doing a good job. They will sit in a seat that is placed at a higher level than yours and look at your forehead instead of making eye contact. They want to show you they are the dominant power. They might look at you over the top of their glasses, belittling toward you.

The way that you can get through a meeting with this type of manager and show your confidence is to picture a flaw about the tyrant and practice negative visualization. Negative visualization is visualizing the faults the tyrant has and keeping them at the forefront of your mind. This will help calm your nerves, because you realize that the tyrant is not perfect, and you likely will be less worried about his or her estimation of you. This will help you in times when he or she is using unkind words and you will be able to get through it unfazed, which will confuse the tyrant because he or she wants to intimidate others. Your body language will be more relaxed once you have pictured the tyrant with his or her faults, and the way he or she is treating you will not bother you as much.

- **The Guilt Monger** – This type of manager tries to make employees feel guilty for not going the extra mile. Typically, the manager will not tell you in a direct manner but will suggest it by pointing out the people who complete that extra step.

These types of managers expect an emotional response from you, and you should not give them that satisfaction. Respond to the task at hand. If he or she only requires a certain amount of work from you and you have achieved that amount of work, then there really is not a problem. Keeping your body language as a relaxed as possible will convey that these managers are not able to affect you, and they will in turn leave you alone. Keeping your body language open and your facial expressions neutral will also convey that they are not bothering you, and will allow you to go about the rest of the workday in peace.

- **The Merchant of Blame** – This type of boss will blame everyone in the office for failed ideas, but never personally take on any of the blame. This person mostly ducks and dodges.

These managers often complain about the poor work you have done on a project that was really their responsibility. If this happens, make eye contact with them and explain how you feel about it in a calm manner. Do not falter when you are making your point, because it might convey uncertainty in how you viewed your role in the project. A falter in your body language would include a shift in your seating position, touching your face while speaking, or fidgeting with an object. If you do not falter, they will be less likely to blame you for the projects they failed, especially once you have maintained a firm position.

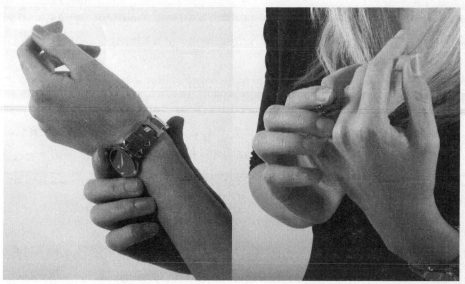

Playing with things like jewelry or a watch can convey nervousness and fear. When communicating with your managers, be sure to keep the fidgeting at a minimum to help you exude confidence.

9. Taking the Time to Listen

Listening is the strongest verbal and nonverbal skill you have, especially because silence can send more messages than words can ever express. Being silent can tell a person a number of different things about you. Here are some tips for active listening:

- **Rely on body language.** When people ask you if you are listening to them, your body language clues are telling them you are distracted or not interested. If you are not talking, then your sense of hearing increases. Try to establish the same focus that you would use if you were to close your eyes while watching television or listening to a song — you will be able to hear the message that they are sending more clearly. Closing your eyes is not possible in a business setting, but, if you are not looking directly at the person speaking, you tend to pick up subliminal messages and hear the inflection in his or her voice a little more clearly. Remember to still maintain some eye contact, though, so the person knows you are listening.

- **Stay silent.** You are able to focus more on the reason the statement is being made. You have a tendency to double the amount of eye contact you make when you are just listening than you do when you are talking. With this, you are able to pay attention to more facial expressions and the hidden meaning behind them. There is a heightened awareness of nonverbal cues during silence.

- **Do not mask your insensitivity to the speaker.** Silence is your best offensive move if you are unable to understand, answer, or just plain do not care about what is going on, and you can easily show that with your body language. A shoulder shrug will let the person speaking know that you do not understand what he or she is saying, or that you do not have an answer for him or her. To indicate that you are not concerned with what is going on, you might also want to cross your arms or legs, or fidget with something nearby. Also, neglect making eye contact with the other person.

- **Sometimes the best answer is no answer.** There are times when people are just looking for someone to listen to them. They will ask you a direct question if they want a response from you. Just as long as you are attentive, most of the time the speaker is content. Nodding your head at the appropriate moments and smiling where it might be needed is a sign of attentiveness toward the speaker and can make the speaker feel as though you are answering him or her without you even having to say a word.

Crossing your arms across your chest and looking away from your co-worker are nonverbal cues that you are not listening; you have closed yourself off from the conversation.

The best communicator usually wins in a business setting. What to say and when to say it is part of the mastery of communication. Comfortably, competently, and articulately speaking to groups of people does come naturally to some people, but others must learn to do this. Knowing when to be quiet and listen is just as important as knowing how to express your feelings, wants, and needs.

A shoulder shrug, a headshake, or staying silent is an important part of listening to the other person. Show confidence with you manager by knowing which type of boss he or she is, and then apply the proper body language in his or her presence, such as relaxed or confident body language, and make the appropriate eye contact. You have to mark your territory with your body language, like leaning back in your chair, crossing your legs, and closing off your body language. You have to know how to handle all kinds of scenarios in the workplace, and being armed with knowledge of the signals your body language is sending is half the battle.

Did You Catch That?

✓ Getting through a meeting without making enemies is crucial in the workplace. Keeping your body language open when addressing issues will help in this matter.

✓ Interviewers not only rely on what you say, but how your body language matches the verbal clues.

✓ Your first day on the job will always be stressful, but walking in with confidence and enthusiasm will help you get through the day.

✓ Meeting a new client can be difficult if you do not know anything about him or her, but building rapport by mirroring his or her body language is important to landing the account.

✓ Showing confidence with your manager can be an important part of getting through the day.

✓ Knowing how to respectfully decline any further contact with a client, colleague, or manager, by knowing the proper body language cues to send, can be an important part of your career.

✓ In order to bond with new colleagues, determine what their personality type is by picking up on their nonverbal cues.

✓ Knowing what to say, and when to say it, is just as important as expressing yourself verbally and nonverbally

✓ Take the time to listen to the other person, both verbally and nonverbally.

CHAPTER 10

Battle of the Sexes

In the context of nonverbal communication, men and women are very different, and thus body language differences between the two are widely researched. Neither gender's body language characteristics are better or worse, they are just different. Learning how to spot these differences — in relation to what message is being sent and how your messages are being received — will help you to communicate better with both genders in the workplace.

Knowing the Difference

Differences in body language appear in everyone, and they are not just limited to cultural differences. In fact, things like gender, age, and social status can also influence a person's body language, and how that person interprets the nonverbal signals of others. Scientists have found that women are able to read body language better than men. A study cited in a research article in the April issue of *Psychological Science* explored the difference between men and women's ability to categorize others based on body language and appearance. In the study, 280 heterosexual, undergraduate men and women examined photos of women and were asked to put them into one of four categories: friendly, sexually interested, sad, or rejecting. The photos that were selected by the researchers clearly portrayed one of the four characteristics. The researchers used test groups to confirm a category (by majority vote) for each woman in the photos. After conducting the study, researchers concluded that women were able to correctly categorize more photos than men did; in some instances, women were nearly 7 percent more likely to read the nonverbal cues in the picture correctly.

Research shows that part of this could be because women typically rely on their emotions more than men, making them more perceptive of other's body language cues. The times are rare when a man's analytical ability or a child's simple wisdom can outwit a woman's intuition when it comes to emotions. Oftentimes, a woman is better trained in nonverbal communication when she becomes a mother and her child is unable to speak. Some women even have an inherent quality that allows them to know just when a child has to use the bathroom during potty training. Their instincts are further enhanced when their children become teenagers who are under emotional distress and clam up when around their problems. These women will know the nonverbal signs of problems within their teenagers' manners. Although men, as fathers, need to know these signals too, women are more naturally in-tune to them, because they are usually better at detecting cues when it comes to the emotions. Men, on the other hand, are typically better at detecting cues when it comes to status.

Why the Difference?

Behaviors and the reason for those behaviors are a part of the noticeable differences in the body language of men and women. The basic survival characteristics are what are known as the preprogrammed elements of nonverbal communication. Passing on their genes, defending their territory, and providing protection are all preprogrammed characteristics of men. Organizing a social environment, nurturing children, and finding a desirable mate, on the other hand, are what are known as the preprogrammed characteristics of women.

The environment you live in and your social influences will shape your culturally learned characteristics. There are differences from culture to culture and from one generation to the next. Achieving success, masculinity, and status are the culturally ingrained characteristics of men, whereas interpersonal aspects of life, connections, and relationships are the cultural characteristics of women.

Although these generalizations about men and women have developed since ancient times, these characteristics are not necessarily true for everyone. Additionally, the development and display of both sets of characteristics are varied greatly in modern life. As stated earlier, women in the business world can take on male characteristics of dominance, assertiveness, and power to achieve the success they desire. Women are typically adopting these characteristics for their survival in the business world, considering that in most cases women are still outnumbered by men. Still, there are women who will participate in the business world without the adaptation of the male characteristics. Emphasizing their own skills, attributes, and contributions usually helps women overcome the male bias in the business world.

Men have also adapted, often blending traditional female characteristics with their own. Long gone are the days when men were not allowed to show their emotions, share their feelings, or nurture children. Instead, these characteristics are seen as highly desirable, because society expects a man to show mutual respect, be part of the relationship partnership, and be an active father. Traditionally, the man was supposed to be the breadwinner and the head of the family. The man being the stay-at-home parent was out of the question 30 years ago, but it is becoming a more frequent choice these days. Ultimately, this helps levels the playing field in the business world. A whole new world of freedom has been opened up for men and women, because now they can express themselves with authentic body language instead of the body language that is expected by traditional standards and customs. Men will not compromise their masculinity if they show caring and nurturing nonverbal behaviors, and women can remain feminine while exuding an assertive and confident body language.

Although this freedom to be authentic is exhilarating, it can occasionally create misunderstandings and conflicts. There are times when simple touches can be misinterpreted. For instance, when someone wants to encourage his or her co-worker, he or she might place a hand on his or her shoulder, which might be interpreted as an intimate gesture. Sometimes high fives and friendly shoulder punches are given when a person is happy, but some people may interpret this gesture as being hostile or aggressive instead of friendly. Both genders are equally capable of sending and receiving any of those signals. Thus, the interpretations can be completely different, which lends to the challenge of body language differences between the genders.

The Difference in Sending

Experts are unsure as to why, but generally women can express subtle nonverbal cues better than men. The experts seem to agree that it could be due to their preprogrammed characteristics of organizing a social environment and nurturing a child. Women are able to influence other people using their ability to express themselves with their body language and nonverbal behaviors without obviously or openly doing so.

Men and women use voluntary body language for very different reasons. Men will use it as a symbol of power and status, whereas women will use it to convey their emotional state. For example, women will give hugs as a routine sign of affection, whereas men will usually only hug someone if they think romance is in the air. Research done by Mark Morman at Baylor University shows that most unconsciously men fear hugging because of stereotypes and a fear of being seen as overly sensitive and homosexual. Therefore, their voluntary body language is to offer a handshake, or a combined hug and handshake.

There are some other differences: Women tend to touch themselves during conversation more than men do, and they also tend to smile more often than men. Women also receive smiles more than men do. Men, on the other hand, will not gaze at each other that much. Although these are helpful generalizations, be sure to take personality traits into account when you are interpreting the nonverbal cues someone is sending you during a conversation at work. When men and women talk to other people about their emotions, the differences are also very apparent. Facing the other person, leaning slightly forward, and using eye contact and facial expressions are all ways women tend to communicate feelings, all of which are also signs of open communication. Turning away from a person, separating themselves with a little bit of distance, or talking while doing something else are all traits that a men typically portray when speaking about their feelings, tending to relate more to closed communication.

Additionally, men will use their body language to communicate power, especially in the business world. Touch, posture, and gestures are all used by men to convey their stature. They use open body language with upright shoulders and a motionless body posture to indicate their confident, capable authority. Those who have a slouching posture, stoop their shoulders, or fidget with something are seen as weak. Trying to project your confidence when you naturally have closed body language is virtually impossible. Women engage in more eye contact than men do, but men use their eyes to communicate power. Women will engage in more eye contact because they want to show the other person they are paying attention.

To be accepted, men and women will take on the body language traits of the opposite sex in order to be successful within a certain professional environment. There are times when you will see women wearing ties that resemble men's fashion. They might even cut their hair in a short, cropped cut, similar to a man's. A woman, for example, might try to appear more relaxed by sitting in a figure four classical male position, or might try to exude confidence and equality by using a firm handshake. All of this leads to a difference in receiving these same body language cues.

The Difference in Receiving

Generally, women are also much better at receiving and interpreting body language and nonverbal messages than men are. Research shows that when it comes to reading body language, spotting inconsistencies between verbal and nonverbal cues, and noticing small details of body language, women are more adept at figuring out the true message.

Experts believe that the preprogrammed characteristic of child rearing has given women the natural ability to sort out the details of body language. From infancy to the age of 2, a child mostly relies on his or her body language to communicate his or her needs, and women, who are usually the primary caretakers of small children, have to learn how to interpret their children's needs and wants accurately.

Different parts of the brain are used in different ways in men and women, and this has been revealed through Magnetic Resonance Imaging (MRI). Women will use up to 16 different parts of their brain when processing and interpreting the messages and behaviors being sent by another person. Conversely, men will process and interpret the messages being sent by another person with only six different parts of their brain. Thus, it can be determined that women read more into the body language signals that others send during conversations in the workplace, and also are more likely to accurately determine what someone is really trying to say. Although some body language occurs involuntarily, women are typically more conscious of what their voluntary body language means, and therefore use body language more efficiently. But, even though MRI research leads to the conclusion that women are better at receiving and interpreting the signals being sent, men are just as adept at reading body language signals once they have learned what certain signals mean.

Being Able to Navigate Between the Two

Knowing the general differences between the ways men and women receive and send messages can be helpful in your next interaction — use these generalizations as a guideline when you walk into your next meeting. Your real life interactions will vary, based on your co-workers' personalities.

When you are building rapport, establishing trust, or negotiating a deal, being aware of the gender differences can be very helpful. When the genders are attempting to mirror each other's body language to build rapport, they will have a better sense of how the other person sends and receives nonverbal cues. Resolving a conflict can also be made easier when you notice and appreciate the differences between the genders.

The next time a difficult situation occurs, use the information provided in this chapter to help you work your way through the problem, remembering the guidelines of gender differences.

Did You Catch That?

✓ Because of preprogrammed and culturally learned characteristics, the differences between the two genders can be great.

✓ Women will use 16 different parts of their brains to interpret nonverbal messages, whereas men will use six different parts to interpret those same messages.

✓ A man and a woman can interpret the same set of events differently.

CHAPTER 11

Personal Relationships in the Workplace

Love and work are two of the basic needs of human beings, according to psychologists like Sigmund Freud, Erik Erikson, and Abraham Maslow. There are similar energies that fuel both of these needs, as explained by the Attachment Theory, which explains the natural connection between human beings. But psychologists have found that this bond is not limited to personal relationships, but also includes work. In the Attachment Theory, exploration is a common theme: In order to learn about your environment, you must explore. However, in order for this exploration to take place, the theory states that a level of attachment must be established. These tendencies of attachment and exploration are expressed in various ways in both love relationships and work relationships.

As both domains are explored, the rewards are the same for both —gratification and affirmation. Emotionally, these rewards come with the stability of the relationship and a feeling of happiness. But, in order to be completely happy in a relationship, there has to be financial gain in another aspect of a person's life, and those rewards are achieved through work. Thus, most people have a tendency to invest more of their time and energy into their work and displays of affection.

Typically, we spend at least 40 hours a week at our jobs, so an office romance easily has the potential to bloom, especially because the attachment to work has proven that the environment is already safe. Though it is prohibited by most places of employment, it still happens. Sometimes it can occur without anyone knowing until that relationship fails, but other times it is completely obvious to the entire office. The potential for a good, bad, or obsessive romance can occur at any moment during company time.

CASE STUDY: A MAGICAL WORKPLACE ROMANCE

Janine and William Lehrer
Longwood, Florida

It is often referred to as the most magical place on earth for families and kids. For Janine and William Lehrer, Disney is the place where they got their start. The Lehrers, married for 22 years, met while working for the Magic Kingdom's parking department.

The two were friends for a while before starting their relationship, which not only marked changes in their feelings for each other, but also in their body language. As they started dating, Janine said Bill would stand as close as he could to her, while Bill noticed Janine's openness to him, which was different from her former rigidness. Although their body language was relaxed when they were alone in the break room or around their friends, they kept things professional when dealing with park guests and other co-workers.

However, the neutrality of their body language at work did not put all of their co-workers at ease about their relationship. Some of them thought Janine would get special treatment because Bill was her immediate boss, and when the upper management team found out that Janine and Bill were engaged, they transferred Bill to another department. Janine said she never received special treatment, and actually found that Bill gave her harder jobs to do instead of the easier ones.

The Lehrers live in Longwood, FL, and have two daughters, 20-year-old Alise and 17-year-old Ariana.

Looking for Love at Work

Most companies have policies against personal relationships within the workplace. These policies are in place for many reasons. They aim to keep relations among employees from being inappropriate and to protect employees from harassment.

Dating policies are also in place to minimize the amount of personal drama and distraction brought to work. The hardest part of the relationship is when it ends, and these same individuals are still forced to see each other every day in the office. They can easily have moments where their bodies tense up, especially when they are approaching one another. Depending on the severity of the break up, sweat may form on their brows and their eyes might narrow. One, or both of them, might leave the company if the tension becomes too distracting.

Perhaps the worst type of dating in the workplace occurs when a superior dates a subordinate. Questions about the motives behind this type of relationship often spring up within the office. People will suspect favoritism and ambition, among other things, from one or both parties involved. These suspicions can result in distractions for both the couple and their co-workers.

It does not matter where we are, the body will unconsciously react to the potential for love. In the workplace, where emotionalism is rejected and professionalism is expected, the body will still react to this force of nature. For example, if a woman and man find each other attractive, their body temperatures rise, causing them to sweat and become warm. These changes are physiological, whereas other responses are psychological, like a woman becoming aware of how she looks and a man adjusting his posture during conversation with the woman.

Love at work can be a problem, even though the yearning for love and work is a natural occurrence. There are companies that have instituted policies against dating in the workplace because of this. No matter what policies may be in place, it does, and will continue to happen. The very first signs of attraction and love can be seen in the body language of the participants.

Attraction in the workplace automatically changes the dynamic and body language of two employees. Here, the romance has sparked a casual, unprofessional sentiment in the workplace.

Flirting

Detecting and expressing attraction toward another person can be obvious through body language. Flirting is the main behavior that will occur — both sexes use their eyes to signal their attraction to the other person. The male counterpart may stare for a prolonged period of time, without blinking at the woman, whereas the female counterpart may bat, or flicker, her eyelids, or give a series of short gazes toward the man.

Flirting can be done through clothing choices. Women choose their clothing, jewelry, makeup, nails, and hair in order to appear more attractive to male counterparts. She will usually accentuate parts of her anatomy in order to appear more attractive. When a man has a deep voice, toned muscles, or a risky job (such as a firefighter or police officer) he might be naturally more attractive to most women. Many women are attracted to a man in a uniform, especially combat gear such as what a soldier would wear, or what police officers and firefighters wear. Men, on the other hand, may find a woman with a nice body or pleasing facial features more attractive.

According to a 2004 study of women's waist to hip ratio (WHR) at the University of Texas, women with a significantly narrower waist than hips are most desirable to men. This WHR of 0.7 or lower is comparable to that of Miss America contestants and Playboy models. However, the same study showed that females with a range of 0.67 to 1.18 are attractive to men in general, while a WHR of 0.8 to 1.0 in men is attractive to women. This level of attraction is subconsciously controlled, and so is the human response to someone who is attractive; it is often automatic.

Although the stance of the male employee in this picture shows a slight discomfort with the forwardness of his female co-worker, his open smile and prolonged stare show that he is open to the flirtation.

Body language plays an important role in flirting — initial flirting begins with nonverbal, naturally occurring gestures. A German ethnologist, Dr.

Irenaus Eibl-Eibesfeldt, was one of the first people to perform a study on flirting in 1960. Scientists discovered that when people flirt, they use submissive gestures that convey they are harmless. The harmless gestures are:

- Placing the palms of their hands on a knee or tabletop
- Tilting their head while shrugging their shoulders
- Being childish or playful

The director of the Center for Nonverbal Studies, Dr. David Givens, discovered that women will make multiple trips to the bathroom during the workday, provided that the person they are interested in has an office in that walking path, so that they can scout and be seen by the opposite sex. This is one of many "notice me" gestures that happen when the first phase of flirting occurs.

Women are better at reading flirtatious signals because they often spend more time perfecting them. Men are oftentimes oblivious to the signals and are seen as less perceptive. Women, according to the Social Issues Research Centre's study on relationships, are the ones who initiate the courtship 90 percent of the time. This might be a surprising figure to those who believe men should pursue women first, but if a man does not want to "strike out," then he will wait for a signal from a woman before approaching her.

A woman being kind and friendly can sometimes be perceived as romantic interest from a man's point of view, and they must be careful not to make this mistake. Men and women use smiling in different ways, and this is typically where the confusion lies. Women will use it to express their mood and men use it as a greeting gesture. It is because of these different uses of the same gesture that the man might think that the smile on a woman's face is a courtship.

A perceptive person can spot an office romance just from the body language of the two individuals involved. If you watch the way they interact with one another, you may notice the closeness of their body positions or that they cannot stop staring and smiling at each other.

As she plays with her hair and keeps a light smile, the female co-worker is welcoming the flirting. The two have decreased the distance between them, making for a more intimate conversation.

There are obvious signs of flirting:

- **It is all about the eyes.** Eye contact is the beginning of the flirting process, like most nonverbal messages. It can be the most powerful and effective way to convey your interest to the opposite sex. Staring and exchanging stolen glances shows interest. Skilled flirters can use direction and the width of their eyes to send the person they are interested in messages.

- **Your smile says it all.** Smiling is an indicator of being attracted to a person. Smiling widely while in the other person's presence and at the mention of his or her name shows an interest in that person. In some circumstances this is a dead giveaway.

- **A soothing voice tone.** In order to sound more seductive, both parties will speak slower. Typically, women will raise their voice to sound submissive, where a man will deepen his to sound more competent and confident.

Along with the indications listed above, there are many other signals that can demonstrate an interest, such as touching, or stroking their hair, giggling, and tilting the head. The article "Quasi-Courtship Behavior in Psychotherapy" by Dr. Albert Scheflen, describes how male and female bodies prepare for possible sexual encounters. These changes occur:

- The person's baggy eyes and sagging skin decrease
- The sagging skin on the body seems to tighten up
- Chests stick out a little more
- Stomachs are sucked in
- Less slumping in posture
- Bodies stand more erect

Both parties continue to hold this posture until they have past one another, and then they return to a normal position. The rejection clues should be obvious to everyone, because the body language will tell you that the advances are unwanted. The person who is avoiding eye contact, closes his or her body language, ignores statements, recoils to the touch, or grimaces is not interested. Surprisingly, people often have difficulty interpreting these signals. Although these flirting gestures and tendencies may seem harmless, they can still be an unwelcome occurrence that can lead to harassment or hostility.

Fixations

A fixation is classified as when a person becomes obsessed with an object or person, usually having to do with pleasure. Freud states that fixations represent an excess or lack of gratification during the five developmental stages of one's life. The fixation equals an unhealthy, disproportionate amount of attention. An employer obsessing about success can cause stress and an employee's fixation on the practice of the business can cause his or her peers to reject the employee and his or her ideas, because of the lack of objectivity.

There are people who fixate on work to attempt to heal themselves from a bad relationship. Sometimes being a workaholic is just a way of life for some people. The spouse of a workaholic can become attached to someone else that will show him or her the attention he or she is lacking at home, which will lead him or her to thinking that this person shares the same feelings. Such fixations can easily occur in the workplace, and are often portrayed by body language. When doing a particular task, for example, a person who is fixated on the project will be alert, as he or she sits with an erect body. The tempo of work is fast, as the employee is productively typing, reading, or writing for the assignment. Intensity is additionally displayed by the overall engagement the employee has with the task at hand, as all other body language is closed off to the outside world.

These same characteristics of fixation can be conveyed as an obsession with another employee, instead of with a project. In this instance, the fixation comes with a negative connotation because it creates distress in the work environment. Here are some signs that an obsession with someone at work might be occurring:

- **You can no longer concentrate, because all you can do is think about this person.** You find yourself daydreaming and doodling more than usual.

- **You want to command every move of the other person.** Your controlling nature gets in the way of productivity and you are anxious and preoccupied with what the person is doing or where he or she might be.

- **You suddenly are having displays of hostility or angry outbursts.** You are unable to separate your personal and professional life.

- **You have become very needy towards this person.** You might not be in love with a co-worker, but you love things about him or her. You stop by this person's desk as often as you possibly can; you call or e-mail with questions that range from personal to professional in nature. The object of your affection is starting to get annoyed with you, but you persist. The only way to get you to stop this irrational behavior is to tell you to go away, but that may never be said so as to avoid hurting your feelings. The person gives you obvious body language signs in hopes that you will understand the hint. Some of these signals are a rolling of the eyes, putting his or her hands on top of his or her head in an impatient manner, a sigh that is quite audible, tapping fingers on the desk, and avoiding eye contact with you.

Here are the steps to overcoming a fixated relationship at work:

- **Regain your composure.** When you fixate on someone else you forget to take care of yourself. Turn your attention to the things you loved or enjoyed before ever meeting this person. Pulling back from the person to get this done is quite acceptable and yields a better emotional balance and a mutual respect is formed. You have to commit to doing this on a mental level. Then, and only then, your body language will begin changing. Your emotional frame of mind will then catch up with all the other changes going on. If you start avoiding this person's workspace, then you will no longer feel the need to go there. If you focus on your behavior, your emotions will follow suit.

- **Turn off your phone (or your computer).** Take part in other activities to stop yourself from constantly contacting this person by e-mail, phone calls, or text messaging him or her.

- **Read this person's body language.** When asking questions of this person, pay attention to what he or she is saying and what his or her body language might be expressing. You can ask your partner a question and he or she can tell you that he or she is just fine, but his or her body language will tell a different story. Get clarification for the signals that you are receiving, but do not force anything. Continue to ask question based on what you are seeing. People can appreciate when you are able to decipher their body language and might even come to you later with their concerns.

Flirting and fixations can both affect the work environment by reducing productivity throughout the day. These activities can cause a major distraction to the recipient, causing him or her to not complete the task at hand. Ultimately, this can cause a loss of work, especially if one of the employees is let go as a result of decreased productivity, and the company will have to overload other employees with the extra work. This, in turn, is bad for the company, and the shareholders see a decrease in production and begin questioning the value of the company.

Did You Catch That?

✓ When you spend the majority of your time at work, an office romance has the possibility of developing.

✓ According to Dr. Irenaus Eibl-Eibesfeldt's study, circa 1960, we often interpret flirting gestures as harmless.

✓ An obsessive relationship stems from a deeper fixation, which can be seen in the aggressive body language this person portrays.

CHAPTER 12

Understanding Cultural and Socioeconomical Differences

Reading body language can be challenging depending on who you are dealing with. There are certain factors that need to be considered, such as culture, and other demographic factors. These things can sometimes complicate properly interpreting nonverbal communication, as in the following scenario.

Bill was a traveling businessman for his company. He had to make a trip to Japan for a meeting that would possibly result in landing the company a large account. Bill did not have time to read up on what gestures were acceptable and unacceptable to the Japanese, which he normally did before going to any foreign country. On the plane, instead of doing his normal reading about the country or the client, he was preparing his presentation. As soon as he stepped off the plane, he got into his rental car and headed over to the client's office. Upon his arrival, the secretary greeted him. He handed her his business card with one hand, like he would to anyone else at home. She gave him an odd look, but Bill did not think anything of it. When he was brought into the meeting room, another woman, who was the new client, greeted him. He presented her with the business card the same way he did with the secretary, and received another odd look. She read it immediately and presented him with her business card, with both hands extended out and palms up. He realized his mistake of not extending both hands and holding his palms up, and hoped his potential client did not view it as a strike against him even though it was considered rude to not present a business card like this in Japan. He immediately knew he should have read about the country he was visiting, and on the client, before coming to the meeting. This was a whole new country, where different gestures meant different things than he was used to.

Of course, this is not a concern only when traveling for a business trip. The United States is a melting pot with a mixture of ethnicities and cultures from around the world, so it is important for workers to understand cultural differences. You can step out of your front door and look around your neighborhood to find a different culture living right next door. How you interpret the body language of someone of a different culture, and how they interpret yours, can be completely different, but being able to realize and understand these differences can be very valuable.

For example, knowing what symbols mean in every culture can be a big help; in America, if we give the thumbs up signal, it means everything is OK, or that something was done well, but in other countries, it can mean something completely different.

This may look like a happy gesture of affirmation, but that is not the case in every country around the world.

In Europe, the same thumbs up signal means the number "one;" in Australia, it means "sit on this;" in Japan it means "man," or the number "five." The shoulder shrug, however, is universal to every country as the "I do not know" symbol. If you place you thumb and forefinger together in a circle with the remainder of your fingers extended, then you have the symbol for "OK," in America. This symbol is perceived very differently in some countries, but it is becoming more well known around the world, partly thanks to American television being broadcast internationally. Within the Mediterranean region, as well as Russia, Brazil, and Turkey, the "OK" symbol is understood as a sexual insult; in France, Belgium, and other European countries it symbolizes "zero" or that something is "worthless"; and in Japan it means "money" or "coins."

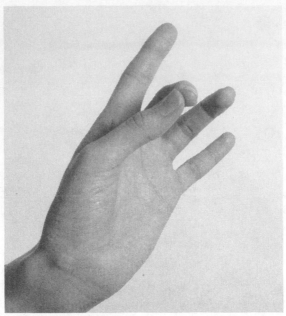

The American symbol for "OK" is interpreted differently in other countries, and should be used with caution.

The "V" we create with two fingers is seen as the number two. If it is created using both arms outstretched, with the palms facing outward, it means "victory" in the U.S., as famously used by Richard Nixon when he won his presidential election. This same hand posture is seen as offensive to the British, because it is a nonverbal way of communicating an expletive. Another example is the different ways Americans wave to greet people. The first way is the entire hand moving back and forth, which in other countries can be misconstrued as something offensive. The second way is with the arm and hand stationary while our fingers wiggle up and down, which too, can be misconstrued as something offensive in other parts of the world.

Facial expressions, on the other hand, are basically interpreted the same worldwide. Universal body language cues and facial expressions are the key to breaking down any language barrier; so, before you travel internationally for business, make sure that you study up on the culture so that you will not offend your business acquaintance, and so you can make communication easier by adding a nonverbal element to any conversation or business meeting.

Race, Ethnicity, and Culture

Spoken language and body language variations are two common differences among many ethnicities and cultures. Not every ethnicity can properly read another race or ethnicity's body language, or understand the spoken language of the other. Facial features and style of dress are the two most common ways you can see these differences. Social attitudes and racial prejudices might hinder a person's ability to understand another person's body language. For example, a study was conducted where college students were tested on facial recognition in infants. Those students who had children or used to baby-sit as teenagers were able to determine what the infants wanted by facial expression alone, whereas those who had never had contact with infants before were usually unable to tell what they wanted. Based on this study, it was concluded that the more contact a person has with someone else, the better that person is at determining what the other person — or a person of a similar age, gender, or race — is feeling. Thus, the more contact you have with a race or ethnic group outside of your own, the better you will become at reading body language.

People tend to pay more attention to the body language of their own race or ethnic group than they do to the body language of other groups, which is why it is important to be aware of how someone's culture and background can affect their body language before going into a business setting with an international client.

Clothing

Clues to a person's culture can be gleaned from their clothing. In Middle Eastern countries, the men wear a headdress and the women wear a hijab. In India, the men may wear a Dhoti, Lungi, or a Kurta, and the women may wear a Shalwar Kameez or a Sari. In the United States, jeans and a T-shirt with tennis shoes are considered normal wear, and most of the clothing worn is made for both genders. Depending on the clothing type, it can be hard to read another person's body language. Certain types of clothing can hide a person's body language, or they can restrict the person's movements enough so that the person does not have the proper body language attached to the emotions he or she is feeling. Take, for example, the Dhoti and Kurta that are typically worn together in India; the Dhoti is a pair of loose fitting pants with a wrap, which can be restricting to body movements because it only allows you to move so far. You are unable to cross your legs in order to tell a person you are not happy with the conversation.

Language and Dialect

There are many different languages and dialects in the United States, but there is a standard dialect. The best place to find this dialect is in the Plains, Northwest, Pacific, and Southwest regions. The Southern dialect is the easiest to recognize because of how Southerners are able to make their vowels stretch from one syllable into two or three. People from the Northeastern region of the United States will often add the letter "r" to some words and drop the "r" from other words. Sometimes a broken English dialect or an accent can be hard to understand. Likewise, it can be hard to understand different dialects and languages because something that means one thing in one language might mean something completely different in another. Language barriers can be an issue when you are trying to form a business relationship. This is why being able to understand body language is important. But, there are variances in every culture and ethnic group.

Although we may rely on them when other means of communication fails, hand gestures can be misconstrued for something offensive and degrading in other cultures and countries even though they are perfectly acceptable in the United States. In Latin America, Asia, and Africa it often is taught that making direct eye contact is a sign of disrespect. In the country of

Denmark, however, the children are taught to make eye contact and shake hands with their elders as a show of respect. In most of the business world and around the globe, it is proper business etiquette to make eye contact, but outside of North America women are, in some places, forbidden to make eye contact with men for a long period of time because it can be seen as flirting or as a sign of interest.

The following is a list of countries and some common etiquette and gestures. This list will help you to conduct yourself with international guests and associates. This section contains general suggestions, but remember every situation is unique and might be different than these guidelines.

- **Australia** – Australians will maintain eye contact during discussions. They keep eye contact throughout the discussion, because they believe it is important to make the other person feel like what they are saying is important to them. They think that business cards are acceptable, and that punctuality is a must. They will give you a firm handshake when starting and ending a business meeting. When they are showing affection, they hold hands, walk arm in arm, or kiss in public. The men generally will not show affection toward their male friends. They will limit strongly expressed emotions; they also avoid the two-fingered "V" hand sign for victory or peace.

- **China** – When conducting business, punctuality is critical, and you must present business cards with two hands. The Chinese will decline gifts at least twice out of common courtesy before accepting them. They never interrupt discussions. The greetings they will give you are a nod, bow, or handshake at the beginning or end of a business meeting. They will not shake hands with people of a radically different social status. They rarely show signs of affection. They believe that putting your right hand over your heart in a horizontal placement shows sincerity. When you move your fingers up and down continuously on a table, you are telling them "thank you."

- **England** – The English value politeness, respect, and punctuality. They will greet you with a handshake. They rarely show affection. They avoid using the two-finger "V" as a sign for peace or victory. They avoid eye contact or staring. They believe that tapping your nose denotes confidentiality.

- **France** – The French always have business cards. They will give you quick handshakes before and after a meeting. When they show affection, they will touch your cheek and they only exchange smiles with their friends. If you want to promise or swear something to them, you place your hands flat on top of your head. If you cover your mouth with your hands, you are apologizing for something.

- **Germany** – Germans will greet with quick handshakes and a slight bow when meeting and leaving a business meeting. They have a large personal zone and will be offended if you enter it. The "OK" hand sign is offensive to them, so they avoid it.

- **Greece** – Greeks will greet you with a handshake and a kiss on the cheek. They will embrace their friends as a display of affection. They will avoid waving goodbye because it is offensive to them — any outward hand motion is seen as offensive. Instead they will give an embrace or handshake and say goodbye.

- **India** – Indians will have business cards and will ask permission before smoking or taking pictures. They will greet you with a slight bow with both palms held together and men will only shake hands with other men. They will not show public displays of affection. You should not touch or pat someone's head or cross your legs.

- **Italy** – Italians will greet you with a lingering handshake or an elbow grasp; they will give you an embrace and kiss your cheeks. They may even hold hands as a sign of affection. The lingering handshake or elbow grasp is an attempt to be in your personal space a little bit longer. An embrace with the kiss on the cheeks is a greeting in Italy, and it is especially used when two people are happy to see each other, or have known each other for some time. They will avoid flicking the chin with four fingers in a sweeping gesture toward another person, because it is an obscene gesture. Depending on the region, Italians decipher the flicking of the chin as "You bore more," "You bother me," "I'm not interested," or "No."

- **Japan** – The Japanese will present their business cards with both hands, palms extended, and they will read yours after receiving them. They will never interrupt during discussions. When they greet you, they will bow and shake your hand slightly. They rarely show signs of affection. They will avoid backslapping or hugging in business situations.

- **Middle East** – Arabs will only use their right hand in transactions, such as eating, greeting, and other daily tasks. This is because the left hand is seen as forbidden and unclean. They will stay within your "intimate zone" while having a conversation. They will have a lingering handshake or grasp your elbow during the handshake. They will hold hands as a display of affection, and they will not point or summon someone with their index finger.

- **Russia** – Russians will greet you with a firm handshake without gloves. It is common practice to wear gloves most of the year. They wear gloves to protect their hands, but upon greeting you for a business encounter, they will show you a sign of respect by taking one off to give you a firm handshake. They will give you a bear hug and a kiss on the cheek. They only smile when they are in the company of friends. They think that whistling shows that you are dissatisfied with something and that laughing loudly is impolite.

- **Spain** – Spaniards will not have their hands in their pockets while having a discussion. They will greet you with a handshake or a pat on the shoulder or back. They will have a friendly display of affection towards others. They will hug each other or put an arm around one another while talking. They will avoid yawning or stretching in public. The men will only sit down after a woman has taken her seat.

- **Sweden** – The Swedish will maintain eye contact during a discussion. They will not interrupt when someone else is speaking. They think that punctuality is a must for meetings. They will greet everyone in the room with a quick, firm handshake, no matter what age or gender they happen to be. They will not show public displays of affection. They believe that sampling everything served during a meal is a polite gesture, and they believe that calling or writing the host the next day is the appropriate way to show your appreciation.

- **Turkey** – Turks will greet everyone present during the meeting. They will have enclosed handshakes. They will embrace someone as part of a greeting. Men will greet each other by kissing each other on the cheek. They will kiss someone's hand as a display of affection. Men who are just friends will hold hands in a public setting. The "OK" hand symbol (placing your forefinger and thumb together in a circle with the remaining fingers extended) is actually a symbol of homosexuality. They will raise their chin, move their eyebrows up, and click their tongue as an indication of "no." They think that shaking your head means that you are not able to understand what they are saying. If you protrude your thumb between your first and second finger, then you are giving an offensive hand gesture.

- **United States and Canada** – Americans and Canadians will greet you with a firm handshake. They will make more eye contact than most other countries. Some people will have limited contact when it comes to affection in public. In Canada, they will not smoke in a public place. They see pointing with the middle finger as offensive.

Age

There are nonverbal clues available to guess someone's approximate age: greying hair, wrinkles, slowed eye movements, softer voice, lighter touch, lower memory capacity, modest and distinctive clothing choices, and an overall slower pace of life.

Although graying hair is a sign of maturity, it can be hereditary, which means that the person will turn grey sooner than normal, so paying attention to his or her body language will be the true indicators of how old the person is. The same can be said for wearing glasses, although, sometimes younger people wear glasses, and there are people who have never worn glasses their entire lives. But, the older a person gets, the slower their eye movement becomes. This can send mixed signals when it comes to sincerity. Older people who are trying to make eye contact to show sincerity may not be able to do so in the same amount of time as younger people. Therefore, it may come off as though they are not sincere because of how long it takes them.

Wrinkles can be a sign of your age, although they can form in a younger person due to heredity or sun exposure. Your emotional expressions can cause expression lines, and might not indicate your age. Those people who have a tendency to smile often will notice the lines around their mouths and a deeper set of lines from their noses to the corners of their mouths. People who frown often might notice the lines that appear in between or above their brows, or a line that appears from the corners of their mouths down to their chins. You might be able to tell the personality types of your co-workers or boss by paying attention to their smile and frown lines, but this is not always an exact indicator of their personality.

Strength also weakens as a person ages. The firm handshake that a business-person may have had in the past might not be as strong as the person ages. It can weaken, due to aging arthritis or lessened strength. Adults touch for many different reasons, but mainly to form bonds with others, such as their business partners. A firm handshake in the business world is important, but the aging process will change the handshake, which may make it seem like the person is not a willing partner.

The way a person uses his or her time changes with age, thus making his or her body language change, too. The youth of the world will rush through things in order to get more done. Younger people also have a tendency to procrastinate. The gestures of the younger generation are often rushed and, often times, too fast for someone to get an accurate read on what that person is trying to say. The older generation is more likely to take their time getting things done, often starting on projects right away and taking their time to complete them as the deadline approaches. Their gestures will be slower and more relaxed, even if they come in bursts that convey the same mental quickness of a younger generation.

However, these natural changes do not always result in lessened nonverbal communication. In many instances, these physical changes result in more sincere and honest body language, exposing any hidden meanings of the eyes, arms, hands, or legs, among other body parts. Age can also increase your understanding of what the nonverbal cues of your co-workers mean — it improves with age and experience.

Wealth and Status

A person's wealth and status can be determined through body language too. According to a study of 100 undergraduate students at the University of California, Berkeley, students of a higher socioeconomic status, based on their parents' income and background, were more impolite during an interview — they were more likely to draw, fidget, or primp at an average of every two seconds. Students of a lower socioeconomic status rarely fidgeted during a 60-second recorded interview clip. Additionally, the students of a lower social status gave off more body language cues to indicate that they were interested and actively engaged in the interview. Thus, the study indicated that people who are of a higher economic status have a stronger tendency to be rude during conversations. These people will doodle, groom, or fidget while talking to someone else, just as the students in the taped interviews did. People of a lower economic class, when spoken to, often to have more polite manners. These people will possibly show more gestures of interest in conversation, such as laughing at the appropriate times and raising their eyebrows. By using these same body language cues, your co-workers and employers will be able to tell your net worth.

Your facial expressions, vocal articulation, touch, movements, style of dress, and the use of your space can all tell another person about your status. A manager will communicate differently with someone who is an employee than with someone of equal rank within the company. You can see this example of communication throughout every social status. Queen Elizabeth, for example, was taught to give a tight-lipped smile, not to be overly expressive, and to conceal her emotions. She was taught this because, for the royal families, showing your emotions is a sign of weakness that makes you vulnerable to your enemies and the public. Not only do those of the upper class have to show poise, but other individuals you might see every day have to learn the value of it. Newscasters are taught to keep their beliefs, attitudes, or emotions hidden, forcing them to have mostly expressionless faces. In this case, a newscaster's face has nothing to do with his or her status. Rap artists will scowl on the covers of magazines and albums to portray the anger and frustration of being brought up from humble beginnings. Based on the backgrounds of your co-workers and employees, you may see some of the same body language cues.

The least common way to distinguish status is through touch. Everyone is capable of violent tendencies, but aggressive behavioral patterns are more common in people of a lower social status. Being gentle and refined is associated with upper class individuals, and the upper class sees being aggressive and rude as characteristics of a lower class individual. The upper class individual might maintain a constant upright body posture and proper manners, whereas the lower class might slouch and not know the proper manners to use when socializing outside his or her class. Wealthy, upper class people might also give their children lessons in etiquette to make sure they can be social with other upper class individuals. The lessons that are learned in these types of classes include proper posture, handshakes, manners, and dining etiquette. Along with etiquette, an appreciation of the arts is instilled in upper class children. The performing arts choice of the upper class is often ballet, which involves graceful movements and touching that translates through their everyday body language.

During the day, you may come across a group of different people at the office and knowing who is in charge by knowing what body language cues to look for will help. In the workplace, you will know when the executives are in the building — they will walk with a tall upright posture and might look down their noses at their employees. When you approach them, they will give you a relaxed handshake; they may possibly fidget with something during the conversation, as if to say that you are wasting their time. They might even mess with their hair while you are talking to them, but their manners are always pleasant. Generally, the social class of the executives of a company is considered higher than those who work for them. Therefore, they are expected to portray their body language to match their status. Likewise, you will want to use the appropriate body language with the people in your office, depending on your workplace hierarchy. You do not want to have the same relaxed and nonchalant body language with an executive as you would with someone who is your friend and on the same power and status level as you. Instead, you want to portray confidence, and a more professional attitude. If you give him or her the same body language as you would someone of your own status, he or she might take offense to it because he or she might think that you are being cocky and seeing yourself as his or her equal, or the executive might consider your informal body language as being nonchalant, conveying that you do not take your job seriously. This can give you a bad reputation amongst the executives and hinder your advancement within the company.

Here are some ways to determine if people have power or high status through their body language:

- They will have large, expansive movements.

- They will keep a tall, upright posture.

- They will have a relaxed, pleasant, and familiar behavior.

- They will turn their back during a conversation.

- They will have comfortable and relaxed, seated positions, such as crossing their legs or having an uneven arm pattern; their body will lean sideways or recline slightly.

Did You Catch That?

✓ Challenges involved in reading someone's body language result from a number of factors: gender, culture, and other demographics.

✓ Men and women use their voluntary body language for a number of different reasons; men tend to use their body language to symbolize their power and status while women tend to use their body language to express their emotional state.

✓ A person's age can affect his or her body language in terms of touch, eye movement, and speed.

✓ Your facial expressions, vocal articulation, touch, movements, style of dress, and the use of your space can tell another person about your social status.

✓ Social attitudes and racial prejudices may hinder a person's ability to understand another person's body language.

CHAPTER 13

Getting It Right — Finding Clues About Signals to
Make the Right Conclusions

It is one thing to be able to understand what each nonverbal gesture or cue means on its own, but when these gestures are used in certain situations, like in the workplace, or with a combination of other nonverbal signals, their meanings can vary. This chapter will help you determine how to tell when you should look for context or cluster cues when applying the knowledge of body language that you have already learned in this book.

Context Clues

Knowing the when, why, where, and who of body language are all context clues. Never examine one gesture for a long period of time to determine its meaning. Instead, take into consideration its motive, the place where it is happening, and your relationship with the person. Rubbing your eyes in the morning has a different meaning than when you rub your eyes in the evening. When you rub your eyes in the morning, it is usually to wake up, but when you do it in the evening, you might be sending the signal that you are tired from a day's work. Likewise, there are many different reasons that people wink, including: deceit, affection, or to give acknowledgements.

Use context clues to determine what it really means when your co-worker winks at you—because there are no other clues in this picture, you do not know if your co-worker is being humorous, acknowledging you, or being deceitful, all of which are possible meanings of a wink.

Another example of when a context clue is needed comes with interpreting cultural body language. In the Middle East, showing the bottom of your shoe is considered an insult, whereas in other parts of the world it is not offensive. Thus, the location where the gesture occurs can play a part in its meaning. A smile done at work or at a restaurant, for example, can mean two different things. If you smile at work, it is usually taken as a polite greeting. If you smile at a restaurant during a date, it might be taken as a romantic gesture.

Not knowing what a gesture's true meaning is can cause you to misread a signal. Stereotyping or generalizing the meaning of a gesture can cause faulty interpretations of a gesture. For instance, someone who is grieving a loss will probably sit with his or her head in his or her hand, but someone who is bored with the conversation taking place might also do this. The person speaking could interpret the gesture as a signal of boredom as opposed to grieving, or vice versa. If you are unsure of the meaning to a gesture, then consult someone that has more experience with the culture of the person you are meeting with. A teacher might have better knowledge of the involuntary gestures children have, and a coach will have a better understanding of the gestures an athlete has.

If your co-workers are resting their head in their hands while you talk to them, it could be a signal that they are bored with what you are saying. But, this same gesture could also mean they are tired or upset — context clues can help you decipher the true meaning behind this.

Nonverbal communication can be better understood if the employees have the knowledge of what the company's background and goals are. Understanding how to speak, gesture, and dress within the workplace is important to create relationships. In order to create a proper business relationship within the workplace, companies institute what is called a "corporate culture," which is simply a company's standard. An attempt at a promotion or retention can fail if an employee does not follow these requirements. The style of dress you choose, such as a short skirt or not showing up with a tie, can send an alarming signal to the managers and colleagues of a conservative company, and be seen as a threat to the culture of the company. Likewise, a gesture can send the same type of alarming signal. For example, a facial expression you used when you were mad at another person or a closed-off stance you had while another person was talking could be a poor reflection on your company's ethical code. You must take into consideration where you are when you are deciding what body language and gestures are appropriate in the office.

Use context clues to determine what it really means when your co-worker is tapping his or her feet — because there are no other clues in this picture, you do not know if your co-worker is bored, anxious, or nervous, all of which are meanings of a tapping foot.

Cluster Clues

Reading the whole body is important when making a decision about what you are going to say or gesture. Gesture "clusters," like context clues, are key to reading someone's body language accurately. This will help in determining whether or not a gesture confirms or negates the verbal communication that it is used with. A person's sincerity can be determined through a smile and hug. A smile alone can mean something completely different than a smile with several different cluster gestures. The smile by itself has the potential to be seen as deceptive, whereas a smile with a hug or a handshake can be seen as a sign of sincerity. Isolating one gesture and examining it might cause someone to come to the wrong conclusion, so it is essential to examine a group, or cluster, of gestures to arrive at the correct analysis. Just because someone is tapping his or her foot does not mean that he or she is anxious or impatient, but if the person is holding the bridge of the nose while tapping his or her foot, then you can assume the person is anxious to move on from the conversation.

Open and closed body languages are the two main instances in which clusters occur. When you are gesturing with an open body language style, you are indicating that you are comfortable, relaxed, or in a composed state. When faced with an impending attack, people tend to leave their body in an open body language to let the other person know that they are ready to fight. The open stance occurs when you leave your arms and legs uncrossed. When you see two men about to confront each other, you will see them walk with their chests out and toward each other. This is commonly considered open body language, but in this particular incident, it is meant as a fighting stance. Other signs of openness exist throughout the entire body. The arms of someone might be moving in sync with the words being spoken. The palms of the hands are often displayed, letting the other person know that there is nothing to hide. The legs are parallel or spread apart. The feet of the person may point outward towards something or someone of interest. A person's eye contact is sustained or prolonged. The clothing of the person hangs freely and there are attempts to loosen or take off some of the attire. Removing a jacket, rolling up the sleeves of a shirt, or unbuttoning a shirt are all signals of an open body language, but in this instance, could signal the start of a fight or argument.

E-body language: Tricks for effective communication when there are no body language clues

These days, a great deal of corporate communication is conducted via e-mail. The problem with this is trying to decipher "e-body language." Unfortunately, employers do not hold lessons on how to interpret online communication. This leaves many workers feeling offended, confused, or just plain irate when a misleading message pops up on their computer screen.

It does not take much to misread the contents of an e-mail. Normally, we can tell the tone of an entire note simply by glancing at the first few words. Let's face it — in the real world, we have the opportunity to craft our words in advance to receive a desired response. This is not always the case with online communication.

Misunderstandings are a common occurrence with e-mail messages.

Keep in mind that any message sent into cyberspace is a permanent document. Once you hit that magic "send" button, there is no limit to who can view your e-mail. If this was not alarming enough, realize that any words of affirmation or praise submitted electronically can have a lasting impact on your reader. Do not be surprised if your kind words reach the hands of the entire workplace during lunch hour. On the other hand, reprimands can make your recipient feel more and more miserable with time.

So how can you avoid sending the wrong message to your colleagues? First of all, be sure you have a clear objective for your e-mail as you write. Always remember that less is more when it comes to conveying your thoughts online. People are more likely to read and comprehend your statements when they are brief and to the point. Never write an e-mail when you are aggravated or out of your element.

Lastly, tone, timing, and tension are key elements to consider in regards to online correspondence. Avoid excessive use of pronouns, such as "you," "I," "me," and "my." Additionally, be sure to steer clear of absolutes, such as "never" or "anything."

In terms of timing, send your note to the recipient when he or she is most likely to respond. No matter what, avoid using childish tactics in your e-mails, such as name-calling or responding to attacks. No one will benefit by escalating any disagreement.

Telling the truth

Insincerity or dishonesty can also be detected when the cluster of body language clues conflict with one another. If a man tells a woman that he loves her, but then stares at another woman passing by, there is a conflict in what he is saying. The sincerity is not there when he says his words. Likewise, when someone says he or she is doing just fine, but the face is telling you the person is sad, the person is not able to talk about his or her feelings.

FBI agents and investigators commonly study body language during case investigations. Although these professionals often couple their detection of body language with lie detector tests, which limit the possibility of answers to various questions to a simple yes or no, the test can only measure so much. Lie detector tests can pick up the heart rate and other biometric levels that indicate whether or not someone is lying, but the facial expressions, nervous fidgeting, and even the sweat forming on the brow of the party taking the test can be indicators as to whether or not the person is telling the truth.

These same nonverbal cues and expressions are also good indications of wrongdoings at the workplace, especially if they are used in clusters. If you have an employee that you are trying to get the truth from and he is sweating, fidgeting, or has an abnormal facial expression, then you probably have a lying employee on your hands and need to investigate further.

Did You Catch That?

✓ Knowing the when, why, where, and who of body language helps you discover the true meaning behind nonverbal clues.

✓ Reading the entire body as a cluster of gestures, before jumping to conclusions, is very important.

✓ Body language is helpful in determining whether someone is lying or telling the truth.

CHAPTER 14

Using your Body Language to be an All-Star Employee

You will come across many situations in the workplace — some negative and some positive. How you respond to them will tell your co-workers more about you. From dealing with co-workers to managers and executives, your attitude toward the situations you encounter can be the cause of your termination or the reason for your advancement. When you learn how to become likable and trustworthy, you will see success within your company. How you deal with the criticisms and reprimands that come your way is an important part of your career. Properly dealing with resignations, firings, company layoffs, and transfers will be a testament to how you truly feel about the company and your co-workers. In this chapter, you will learn about some of the best ways to respond to both negative and positive situations that occur in the workplace, as well as the body language you should use to aid your response.

Likability — Being Open

Bryan had only a high school diploma when he began working in the mailroom at a brokerage firm. Throughout the day, employees would look forward to seeing Bryan because he had ingratiated himself with all of them. The heads of the company noticed his charm and intelligence and everyone liked him. Over the years, he was offered opportunities to advance, even though he did not have a college degree. Within 12 years, he became the CEO of the company.

Bryan most likely developed a winning personality at an early age — one that helped him advance in the brokerage firm — unless it was his ambition that propelled him to success. Your personality alone can sometimes make all the difference. Sometimes, business deals are made because of the winning personality of the company representative.

There are people who have bad attitudes who will succeed in the business world. But, that attitude might not always have been there; it could have developed over time. Some companies only focus on the means and the outcome of the work being done, not on how it gets done, as long as it is handed in on time and done right. There are some companies that prefer a person's performance rather than his or her personality. Bryan is an example of a person who had both the performance and personality many companies look for. Regardless of which type of company you work for, being likable and open will often help you respond to any workplace situation, whether it is with your co-workers or your employers.

According to researcher J.K. Burgeon, the likability for a man in a dominant position is much higher than that for a woman who is in the same position. Usually, even though the level of power is the same, body language will differ between men and women in high-level positions in the workplace. For instance, a man might keep his body language in the open position, with uncrossed arms and legs and a relaxed posture, whereas a woman might be more closed off and submissive, with crossed arms and legs, a slight tilt to her head, and an upright posture. The woman's body language restricts communication between the two parties, so it is less likely to be accepted. Therefore, men in supervisory positions are often seen as more approachable, and ultimately more likable, than women. When women keep their body language open their employees tend to see them as friendlier and more understanding, which increases their likability.

Regardless of your level of authority in the workplace, there are certain body language cues that you can use to portray a likable personality, which can help defuse any situation. A broad toothy smile may not always be the norm in a professional environment, but a quick smile is welcomed anywhere. If you go a whole day without smiling at all, you will be seen as rigid and inflexible, and will probably end up with a nickname that associates you with being stone-faced.

Another tactic you can use is a slight touch to build rapport — this can also help you become more likable in the office, as it adds a personal touch to the conversation, just as long as the touch is not a cultural violation or of a sexual nature. There are people who will guard against acceptance. Those people are known to be impersonal and standoffish. Their personal contact zone is wider than most and they see touch as unwarranted, and possibly see a question as an invasion of their privacy. This can also be seen in their handshakes — they will use two different types of handshakes, one being weaker, conveying that they are not interested, or the stiff-arm handshake, forcing you to stand back.

Sometimes, the clothing that is worn around the office will tell you who wants to be left alone. The people who do not care if they are accepted will wear nontraditional office clothing, which will reflect their rebellious nature. These people usually will have closed body language, with closed arms and legs and minimal eye contact (if any at all), and they will fidget with something or touch their face while having a conversation.

If you are treated warmly and are invited to after work meetings, then you are sending the appropriate signals and are well liked. If you are not being treated warmly, evaluate what your body language is saying to your co-workers so that it does not create a problem while you are in the office.

Trustworthiness — You Will Always be in High Demand

Janet had worked for her company for 20 years, even after they cut her pay and benefits to save the company from going into financial ruin. Within two years, the company became profitable again and Janet was given a promotion, a raise, and a bonus because the company recognized her dedication.

As a result of the economic crisis of 2008, U.S. corporations were forced to outsource, downsize, and restructure in efforts to increase profits and cut expenses. Morale and productivity were affected by these practices as many employees found themselves in positions similar to, or worse than, Janet's. People lost trust in the companies they worked for. What was a business decision on the corporation's part hit too close to home for some, making the decision to lay off hundreds of employees a bit more personal. According to Allen Center, author of *Public Relations Practices*, employees in these companies have a weakened sense of loyalty toward their employer because these companies view their employees as expendable liabilities.

However, employees who could prove that they were trustworthy could sometimes save themselves from being laid off, or could manage to regain their status and salary after a temporary cut, like Janet. Thus, these employees took themselves off of their employers "expendable" list. Some leaders prefer loyalty over any other quality of their employees. Office managers and executives must be able to determine the loyalty of those in their inner circle, especially when the work environment is more serious than an average desk job. Loyal employees are often given "dedicated service" awards and accolades from other types of business.

In the situation with Janet, she would encourage feedback and listen to what was being said. She would smile and show her appreciation to how she was being treated. She would always make direct eye contact with the person who was approaching her. She would always move closer to a person she was having a discussion with and touch or pat him or her to express her reassurance.

Another body language signal you can use to portray your honesty and trustworthiness is placing your hand on your chest — this is a signal for loyalty. Nonverbal communication is the most reliable way to detect whether a person is loyal. If a person is untrustworthy, he or she is not going to tell you. When a person is being disloyal to a company, there are body language signs. *For more information about how to tell if someone is lying, see Chapter 3.*

Handling Criticism

Jill was fresh out of college and beginning a new job, so she expected to be criticized for the first few weeks. As with any opportunity, she saw this phase as a time to improve her skills. She was always willing to learn new ways of doing things, and she took criticism as a way to help further her career, as she listened to her colleagues and superiors with open body language, an understanding nod, and steady eye contact. As the days on the new job went by, she received less criticism from her fellow co-workers, as well as her supervisors and executives. She was really enjoying her job and found out through office gossip that everyone seemed to like her. She knew that the way she received the criticisms from her co-workers had helped in proving that she was going to be good for the company.

There are always complaints or criticisms in any type of relationship, and employment is no exception. The boss of a company will write an evaluation as a formal manner of rating an employee's performance on the job. A supervisor will be known for correcting an employee in an informal matter while he or she is working. There are some co-workers who will offer their advice or even critique another person's performance in order to help them out. Most employees have many ways to get feedback, as Jill was able to get her feedback in her new job. For instance, office gossip can tell how well a particular employee is performing, or if that person is even liked by the rest of the office.

Some people see being critiqued as an affront to their character or ability to do their jobs, but others, like Jill, see it as a avenue to personal growth. This phase will offer you the perfect opportunity to make any necessary corrections or adjustments to further your success. How well you are able to handle criticism will determine whether you receive more criticism. No one likes to deal with defensive people. There does not even need to be a verbal response toward the criticism — the body language of the person being criticized or reviewed will show the hostility he or she is feeling. Even before something is said to him or her, the body language of that person will convey a "stay away" message. When it is determined that verbal correction is ineffective, then a written warning will probably be issued that will permanently be in that person's file.

There are also people who are overly critical, and there is no one or nothing that can please these types of people. Everyone can easily tell that these people are bothered by the constant look of aggravation they wear on their faces. A passive person who is also critical, on the other hand, will only display this with his or her body language. He or she will show some form of anxiety, such as puckering his or her lips, shaking his or her head, or staring at the employee in question. For an aggressive person, the response to criticism is more obvious — both verbal and nonverbal forms of communication will be used, usually to convey the person's dissatisfaction with the criticism he or she is receiving.

Maintaining an open body language, while giving or receiving criticism, will convey that you are friendly and listening to what the other person is telling you. You must be careful about how your unconscious facial expressions might react to the criticisms you are receiving. Sometimes these defensive expressions, such as a frown, raised eyebrows, crossed arms, or other closed body language, are just a part of your normal behavior and cannot be helped. There might be times when people are constantly questioning your mood because of a certain expression. If this is the case, then practicing your reactions or speeches in a mirror will be a big help when trying to handle criticism on the spot.

Responding to Reprimands

Reprimands are usually emotionally charged because they come after a major offense has occurred. Once you have grown up, you do not expect the same type of reprimand you may have received as a child. However, there are those adults who will treat you like a child by screaming, yelling, and even pushing you. Other people might use what is known as emotional blackmail and can completely withdraw their attention from you. Even though there may have been an infraction, there is no reason that an employee should face humiliation, degradation, or alienation. When the reprimand is occurring, the employee's morale, reputation, and self-esteem should always remain intact.

Reprimands that never come are the worst ones to receive, but these can be common in a work environment. Usually, the boss acts as if there is nothing wrong with an employee's job performance by smiling and joking with him or her, as if not to disrupt the flow of productivity or create tension in the office. There is no change in the boss' body language, so the employee thinks that he or she is doing a good job, until he or she is called into the office and told that he or she is being fired. When the employee questions the reason for this action, then he or she is told about several infractions that have happened. The employee becomes confused because his or her boss had never mentioned any of these things until now.

The boss, in this situation, might not be the proper person to reprimand the employee because of his or her personality and friendly relationship with the employee. A mediator would have been able to handle this situation better.

How things are said is one of the most important things when it comes to giving and receiving reprimands, but there are some bosses who prefer to send a message in writing to their employees. However, that written message lacks the voice modification needed for the employee to understand his or her wrongdoing. The message can be interpreted incorrectly because of how the person reading it might have been feeling when they read the message. For instance, if you read the following two sentences three times each, changing the pitch of your voice from mild to average, then to harsh, you will understand how every person can interpret things differently:

- I did not like it.
- I liked it.

More important than the message itself is the employee's response to being reprimanded. The employee who receives the reprimand should seek out an understanding as to why it was issued more than anything else. When the reprimand is done in writing, you should ask for a meeting to get the clarification you need on the specific points of concern. If this is the case, take some time before asking for a meeting to prepare yourself, mentally and physically. It is important that you go into a meeting where you will be highly criticized with an open mind and open body language. However, if the reprimand is done in person then try to read the person's body language and ask the appropriate questions to get the clarification needed, but be careful not to seem like you are challenging your boss's decision. Avoiding closed-off body language that shows you are on the defensive will be a key element in handling the situation properly. An overreaction, in which you would display this type of closed body language, can damage your professional relationship and might ultimately cause a loss of your job. Formal complaints should be used when you feel you have been mistreated or unfairly targeted.

Handing in Your Resignation

Most employees will contemplate resigning for a while before finally deciding to quit. But there are some employees who quit a job impulsively, following situations that they feel are intolerable. Resignations, whether on the spot or premeditated, create a void in the company that must be filled. Companies have to find a suitable replacement, which will cost the company money in both advertising the position and in time, especially for the amount of training needed for the new employee. Until the new employee becomes familiar with the company's services, products, or functions, the productivity of the other employees will be negatively affected. Always try to give an employer a suitable amount of time to find your replacement before you quit; even though two weeks is what may be required, a longer amount of time can be more helpful and less stressful for your fellow co-workers.

There are employees who will quit a job in a contentious fashion, believing that the employer only deserves two weeks — or less — of notice. But, what they fail to realize is if they are on a job for more than one year, they are going to need a reference from the company when applying to other jobs. Always be aware of the manner in which you decide to leave your job. Let your boss and the company know that you harbor no resentment toward them by working harder in your final days, smiling, and expressing an open body language. In your final weeks before your departure, let them see that you are leaving amicably and it might bring them to giving you a better review. Focusing on your future job opportunities, rather than the past, will allow your body language to express pleasure rather than any disdain you may have.

Are You About to be Fired?

Getting fired can come as quite a shock, but before termination occurs, the actions of a supervisor or other employees will probably show their disapproval. There are obvious signs that you are about to be terminated, aside from your boss having closed body language toward you:

- You are getting less work, but your job responsibilities have not changed.

- You are training someone to be your new assistant.

- You are told that it is OK if you leave work early on a hectic day.

- You are told that you may take a vacation during the busiest time of year.

- Your boss will have a conversation with everyone else about job duties.

- You are kept out of the loop when it comes to important company changes.

The body language of the entire office will change toward the employee who is getting fired; there will be less professional and personal interaction with this person. Thinking that the boss is having personal problems, the employee might ignore the sudden change in body language and attitude. This type of distancing behavior should never be ignored. When the effected employee realizes this behavior is occurring, he or she should ask the boss or the other employees if it is because of his or her job performance. During the conversation, the employee needs to pay close attention to the verbal and nonverbal cues being given. Knowing if the verbal and nonverbal messages were consistent, deliberate, or unintentional is an important consideration to get the clarification needed before the termination occurs.

It can be difficult to find work after employment has been terminated, because the employee may not receive a good reference from his or her former employer. The interview takes on even more importance in this situation. The employee must convince the interviewer that he or she was wrongly terminated from his or her previous position. The interviewer will be paying close attention to the body language of the employee during the discussion of sensitive issues, such as former employment and salaries, so it is imperative that he or she is open and honest about these issues, and that the same honesty is reflected in the body language.

Coping with a Layoff

According to the Bureau of Labor Statistics of the U.S. Department of Labor, in the 24 months from December 2007 to December 2009, there were 51,154 mass layoffs that occurred, resulting in 5,187,170 people filing claims for unemployment. Each action involved the layoff of at least 50 people from a company. In an economy where layoffs of this magnitude are the norm, these numbers are not very surprising. Companies reporting the loss of profits, or seeking to make higher profits, will reduce their staff size to compensate.

Even though mass layoffs are not personal, employees who are cut often still feel a sense of loss or bitterness toward their former employer. But, focusing on what is needed to move on, instead of focusing on the past, should be the priority of the former employee. Creating a new or updated résumé, obtaining further training, attending networking functions, finding alternative health care options, and making personal financial adjustments, should all be the main focus of the former employee so he or she can find employment in a minimal amount of time.

A laid-off employee is going to need the support of his or her close family or friends while figuring out the next step. There are chances that depression will strike the former employee without being aware of it; therefore, his or her loved ones will be unaware of it happening. Some people will wait until they receive a verbal assertion before confirming that they were aware of the depressive state the employee was in. There are significant changes in body language that will occur when someone is depressed. Here are some of the signs to look for:

- Social isolation and generally closed body language
- General lack of enthusiasm ·
- Staring blankly at insignificant objects

Companies should have a counselor available to the people that are being laid off because then it will seem like they are empathizing with their employees.

When you are dealing with a layoff, there is no need to scream at the messenger. People have a tendency to get angry at the person who is divulging the information when he or she is not the one who made the decision. It is generally the manager or executive's choice of who gets laid off and it may not have anything to do with your job performance. The direct supervisor is normally feeling the pressure from higher management to reduce his or her team, so making the decision on whom to let go is just as painful for him or her as it is you. Even if you are justified in feeling upset, unleashing your anger on the human resources person or whoever has been assigned to hand out the pink slips will make you look unprofessional. Keeping your hands by your side when you are receiving the information is important. If you throw items, pound your fists, or assault the person who is laying you off, you will be thrown out of the building before you are able to retrieve your belongings. Additionally, when you are hearing the news, try not to be overly emotional. Crying, avoiding eye contact, or snatching the information from the messenger's hands is not going to get your job back. Making a gracious exit and focusing on your next career move or personal goal is the only way to properly leave the building.

Transferring to Another Department

A formal request for a transfer takes plenty of thought. If the requested transfer happens to be declined, then the employee is left to deal with whatever situation he or she was trying to get away from, or he or she fails to gain the opportunity for advancement that awaited in another department. If this is the case, the employee might begin harboring negative feelings toward the job, which could show up in his or her attitude and approach.

Disappointed employees must find something positive about the situation, because extreme emotions are difficult to mask. Your body language will tell everyone about the negative feelings you are having, even if you are not expressing those feelings verbally. Recognizing and changing your negative body language will help change your mood — how you carry yourself affects the way you think and feel. If, even after your transfer is denied, you keep smiling, you will feel like smiling more. If you keep your arms uncrossed, then you will open your mind. Lowering the pitch of your voice will make you feel calmer. Upgrading your attire will help you to gain more confidence. It all comes down to how you choose to handle the situation, and how you choose to train your body — nonverbally — so that you can unconsciously react in the appropriate manner.

Did You Catch That?

✓ Mirroring body language to build rapport, with quick smiles, slight touches, and open body language, will create likability in the workplace.

✓ Encouraging feedback, making direct eye contact, smiling to show your appreciation, and moving closer to a person during a conversation can indicate that you are trustworthy.

✓ When resigning from a position, work harder, smile, and keep your body language open to convey the fact that you have no resentment toward your employer.

✓ Paying close attention to the body language of your boss and fellow co-workers will give you hints as to whether you will be terminated.

✓ Do not scream or be overly emotional when being informed about a layoff. Instead, keep your hands flat or by your sides and stay calm.

✓ When a transfer is denied, thinking about something positive will change your body language, so you will not show your resentment.

CHAPTER 15

What You Can Learn from the Masters of Body Language

There are people in the public eye who are considered masters of body language. Some of them are in the public eye more than others, but they all have figured out a way to convince us to believe what they are saying. This not only has to do with speech, but with their body language. They have a way of making others feel what they are conveying through their words and the movements that go along with it.

Our governmental figureheads, politicians, performers, police officers, and priests or pastors all use body language as a means to make their audiences feel and understand their messages. The masters of their professions use body language to evoke any emotion, from sheer joy to heartbreak. Take a tip from these masters — use their tactics to help you use body language to convey your true meanings in the workplace.

Politicians

Using body language to complement verbal messages is skillfully done by political figures. To ensure that their word choice is perfect, they will use speechwriters, but conveying the whole message goes a step further. They have to come across as caring, yet authoritative, as they are speaking to the general public, so any gestures that suggest deception must be avoided.

This includes things like avoiding eye contact of the press and public and holding the hands behind the back. During live television debates, the body language of politicians is closely watched by body language experts to detect inconsistencies with the verbal and nonverbal messages being sent.

During the 2008 presidential election, body language expert Karen Bradley opined that Senator John McCain represented stability because he stood firmly at the podium while holding on to the sides of it, whereas Senator Barack Obama had a forward gaze while he strolled about the stage when addressing the audience. This gaze, however, was an indicator of a glimpse into a future of change, which was consistent with Obama's message.

Bradley and her consultant, Karen Studd, noticed other differences between the gestures of McCain and Obama. Obama's hand gestures suggested that he was being accommodating to both parties, whereas McCain's directional gestures suggested that he was trying to bridge a gap. How both candidates walked was noted as different by the experts. McCain had a side-to-side swagger to his walk, shifting from left to right, and Obama had a more centered way of walking. According to Bradley, during the live debates, Obama was very relaxed and McCain's stiff, immobile body language made him appear as though he was searching for an escape route.

There are some common nonverbal messages and signals that can be associated with political figures. As previously described, the main messages a political figure usually aims to convey include openness, honesty, sincerity, and competence. The main signals used to express these messages are facial expressions, eye movements, touch, body gestures, vocal intonations, and attire. In the business world, these same nonverbal signals are used to help employees communicate with their bosses.

Performers

A good actor knows that human emotions are mainly communicated by facial expressions, so body language is a key element in the determination of whether he or she is good or bad actor. Facial expressions and gestures have to be congruent with the delivery of the lines. If the actor is effective at combining nonverbal and verbal forms of communication, the audience will forget that they are watching a movie and believe they are watching something that is happening in front of them. Some actors will cause an audience to scream in fear, yell in indignation, or cry in sympathy. Dakota Fanning can pull off an emotional performance, even though she is young and relatively inexperienced. She was in *I am Sam, The Cat in the Hat, War of the Worlds, Charlotte's Web* and *The Secret Life of Bees.* She may only have been 5 years old when she started acting, but she can put on such a performance that she can tug at your heart stings. The body language she conveys when she is putting on an emotional performance matches perfectly with the lines she delivers. This is true for most actors and actresses — at least the ones who can make you believe they are really their character. When the actor is sad you will see it in his or her facial expression — his or her eye movement will be directed toward the ground; he or she will have a slumping body posture; his or her voice will be quiet; and his or her attire may be wrinkled or tattered.

Other performers, such as musicians, use body language to help them enhance certain emotions, too. In the case of musicians, a record label will groom the artist's image for the most appealing public presentation. How the public perceives an artist determines how his or her image is described, such as, "sexy," "sweet," or even "crazy." Often, this can be done during a photo shoot with careful placement of the arms or legs, or with art direction for a certain type of eyes. Again, body language is essential for creating the proper feel. The main messages that performers need to portray often require using their facial expressions, eye movements, body gestures, vocal intonations, and attire to convey their feelings.

CASE STUDY: LET THE MUSIC TAKE CONTROL; BODY LANGUAGE OUTSIDE THE WORKPLACE

Charles Boyer, musician
5 Billion Dead

Charles Boyer has been a part of Orlando's local music scene for the past 4 years. He is currently the lead singer of a band call 5 Billion Dead (**www.myspace.com/5billiondead**).

Boyer believes that as a musician, he needs to understand the basics of body language in order to help his band succeed. As the front man, he has to be able to read the crowd and pump them up when they look a little lackluster. Likewise, he is able to match his body language to the music by feeling it. When the music is aggressive, he acts accordingly, and when it is mellow he will relax himself. The audience relies on the band, as a whole, to get them excited, and to keep them that way. The audience will pick up on their every move, even if they do not realize they do it. The audience's reaction is all that matters to Boyer. He has to pay attention to how they respond and what they do not respond to.

Portraying the raw emotions of the music involves his entire body and the way he carries himself. When he is performing a sad song, that emotion will translate trough his facial expressions and his slumped body language. He likes to let the memory of the emotion he used to write the song take over his mind, then allow his body language to naturally portray that feeling. He has had people express to him how they felt when he was performing a certain song, so he believes that the audience understands and is able to read his body language.

However, the ability to use and read body language during a performance is not always an advantage for a musician. Some people try to create a certain way of expressing themselves on stage, Boyer said, and that comes across as contrived to many people, but the musicians who let their movements flow from their feelings inside have an effect on people. His stage presence is 50 percent due to the audience's body language and 50 percent his own craft. But, he relies 100 percent on his own feelings to create the appropriate body language for the song he is singing.

Royalty

Some public figures need to adopt nonverbal signals as a part of their heritage, while others consciously adopt those same behaviors. The wedding of Prince Charles and Camilla Parker Bowles contained no embrace or kiss. When they left the church, they left with tight-lipped smiles and their arms locked within each other's arms. Even though the couple had just been married, no one was able to tell, because of their lack of public displays of affections. The public had only seen an expression of class that was exuded through restraint, which is exactly what the newlywed couple wanted the public to see.

Portraying class and poise is demanded of members of the royalty. When a common person comes in contact with a member of the royal family, he or she must bow or curtsey. In ancient Chinese tradition, citizens would receive punishment for not performing the strict nonverbal protocol when coming in contact with royalty. Women had to have pleasant expressions on their face when in the presence of the emperor. When men met the emperor, they had to perform the "koutou," which had strict guidelines. They had to perform a right and left sleeve brushing ritual from the top of the shoulder to the tips of their fingers, bend down, place one knee on the floor, a right hand on the back, and their hand had to hit the floor. You can still see these actions being performed in movies, and it is still expected in certain parts of China. Through this practice and use of body language, Chinese commoners were able to demonstrate their respect and loyalty. Although you would probably not greet your boss in this same manner, more modern uses of the body can portray the same feelings of respect and loyalty, such as standing when you shake his or her hand, sitting with an erect posture during a meeting, or reducing the amount of fidgeting you do in your boss's presence.

The main messages that royal figures must portray, on the other hand, are politeness and power. The signals used to express these messages are facial expressions, eye movement, body gestures, and attire. The facial expressions of the royal families are generally tight-lipped smiles, if any smiles at all, or an expressionless face, with minimal eye movements and body gestures, matched with an impeccable wardrobe. You can utilize all of these nonverbal cues in your workplace body language, especially when it comes to dressing for the job you want. You should always maintain a polite and professional attitude to help you get that promotion you desire.

Police Officers

When faced with a chaotic situation, police officers must remain calm. When there is danger coming at them, they must remain courageous. When there is an air of suspicion, officers must remain objective, meaning mastery of both verbal and nonverbal communication is required. An officer has unique and distinguishing body language. A commanding presence, stance, personal space, and eye contact are all a part of an officer's body language. A command presence is acting, appearing, or being calm, cool, professional, and in control, even if you do not feel any of those things. Keeping their backs straight, their heads held high, arms out, with their feet wide apart and one foot back are all a part of what police officers learn in the academy. Aside from wearing clean, pressed uniforms with their shined weapon belts and shoes, an officer must walk with a purposeful stride, use direct eye contact, and have a strong voice — all things that convey power and authority nonverbally. Officers need to anticipate any sudden movements so they will keep their weapon hand free. Additionally, an officer's eyes are constantly roaming around an area to scan for possible threats.

The main messages an officer must portray are authority, dominance, and competence. The signals that they use to convey these messages are facial expressions, eye movement, body gestures, and vocal intonation. The facial expressions of an officer must remain neutral during a suspicious or chaotic situation. The eye movements of an officer will be constant, more so than normal, because they are looking for danger. They will have an erect posture and a commanding stance, giving off a strong presence. As you have learned in this book, all of these nonverbal cues give off signs of power, authority, and confidence.

Priests and Pastors

Some religions can be identified by a description of what its practitioners wear and how they behave. For example, Judaism advocates modest dress and behavior. The Hasidic Jews are perhaps the most distinctive sect of this religion, as they dress to prove that their faith separates them from others. Males have long beards and dress in black, often with a black hat. Not all Hasidic Jews dress like this and this branch of Judaism is just one example of a unique dress and behavior of the many religions of the world.

Although some religions uphold traditional dress standards, nowadays, the pastors of some churches have relaxed their traditional attire for a more casual look in an effort to make parishioners feel more comfortable with them and the message they are preaching. Again, you can apply this ability of certain religious leaders to your everyday job in the workforce: Dress for the message you are conveying.

More important than garb, however, is the practice of love and community that is encouraged within most religious groups. The Christian community, for example, expects parishioners to make certain sacrifices, such as their time, talent, and/or money to help support others in their community. As the head of the church, the pastor must set an example for his or her parishioners to follow. In other words, he or she must act in a way that conveys caring and concern toward his or her fellow man. Smiling, shaking hands, and affectionately touching people are all a part of being a priest or pastor.

Throughout the religious community, there is another virtue that must be expressed: humility. In order to convey this virtue, a person will reduce his or her height and increase distance from another person. Kneeling, bowing, or lowering your head while praying is associated with paying respect. In the Islamic religion, for example, it is common practice for worshipers to bend at the waist, or bow, repeatedly while praying. Additionally, priests and pastors often use their facial expressions, eye movements, and body gestures to portray these messages to their parishioners. When giving their sermons, priests and pastors will use their facial expression in combination with their eye movements and body gestures to emphasize their message. The same sentiment can be gathered from examining the body language of these religious figures — it is not just about what you say, but about how you say it. Therefore, using body language in the workplace is often essential, as you have learned.

Did You Catch That?

✔ Politicians must convey openness, honesty, sincerity, and competence, all through their body language.

✔ Performers must make you believe that they are actually experiencing the emotions they are portraying through their body language.

✔ Royalty will portray politeness and power through their body language.

✔ Police officers will show authority, dominance, and competence through their body language.

✔ Priests and pastors convey humility, caring, and competence through their body language.

CHAPTER 16

Reading Your Own Body Language

Your thoughts, feelings, emotions, attitudes, and self-confidence are all expressed through your body language. But, knowing what nonverbal messages you are sending and how they are received and interpreted by others can be beneficial. Impressions can be made about you through your nonverbal cues. Making choices about when, where, and how to use different body language cues will be easier once you have greater awareness of what nonverbal cues you are sending. Once you know which behaviors are serving you well, you can determine when to use them more often. And, once you figure out which ones are hurting you, you can then make a conscious effort to change them. Knowing your personal identity or your status will help you to make adjustments in your behavioral patterns to suit every situation that life has to offer, especially in the business world.

Ways to Know your Personal Identification

Your personal identification defines how others see you — it is unique to you. Through use of your body language, you can establish your personal identification, making it your signature; everyone will remember the statement you made when you walked into the room.

For instance, say you want your personal identity to be as an executive at the Fortune 500 company you are currently working for. You can see yourself running the company, and you enjoy knowing everything there is to know about the business world. This will become evident through your body language. You may start to walk with your head held high when you are at the office, indicating that you know the ins and outs of the company — or at least you think you do. You will walk with confidence throughout the day. When you are in a meeting or around the executives of the company, you might mirror their body language, sending them the body language cues that identify you as one of them.

Another example of personal identification is becoming the shy person in the office. Deep down, these people may be afraid to get hurt or ridiculed, so they will keep to themselves and not really talk to anyone. They are known as loners and may not have many friends, but they will do their job efficiently and effectively. You will probably see them move their bodies away from people when they are passing by in the hallway, or avert their eyes from making contact. They might smile only rarely, and often have closed body language. They will hide their fears and emotions as much as possible, which is what contributes to their personal identification.

Remembering that your body language is constantly telling people about your attitude, feelings, thoughts, self-confidence, and emotions will give you the power to change the behaviors that may be hurting your career. You might cycle through different personal identities throughout the day; most people do. When you are aware of what your body language says about you, then it will be much easier for you to make the choice to keep, alter, or abandon your nonverbal behaviors in order for you to achieve the success you are after.

Are You Confident?

A confident body language is easy to spot, but it can also be the easiest body language to fake, even when you are not feeling it. A smooth, steady stride, without hesitating or pausing along the way, is the walk of a confident person. These people will always have an upright posture, with their shoulders back, heads up, and their eyes focused straight ahead. The person who exudes confidence will have a steady voice and steady hands.

If you deliberately make the necessary behavioral changes to exude confidence every day, then your mind will develop the confidence you need.

Your performance at work may have caused you to be extra confident one day, but if you are unsure how your body language appeared during a presentation you were giving or meeting you were in, you can ask a co-worker. You might find that you did not look confident at all — your hands were shaking, your shoulders were slumped, and you were avoiding eye contact. This means you might have to work on getting your body language to match what you are thinking.

Faking confident body language might be necessary sometimes. The first day on a new job can make you feel scared, excited, nervous, and anxious all at the same time, but you want to appear confident the first time you step foot in the door, so you fake a confident walk. This action made the office think that you are capable of getting the job done. You knew you had to keep your posture upright, your head up, and you had to walk down the hall to your new office with a smooth motion.

When a person is unsure of himself or herself, on the other hand, his or her body language makes it quite obvious — a hesitant emotion radiates. Darting eyes and hesitant movements are the nonverbal cues that accompany being unsure. When people are unsure of which direction to go, or they lack confidence in what they are saying, you will notice that their eyes may dart around the room. In the business world, the prominent speaker during a meeting will dart his or her eyes around the room to meet everyone's gaze in order to ensure that his or her message is being received. When an unsure person is speaking to another person, his or her eyes may dart from the person's face to the floor and back again, hoping for some reassurance. If that person does not get the reassurance he or she needs, then his or her eyes will probably continue to dart around the room, seeking an escape route.

When a person is hesitant, his or her movements will not be smooth or steady. This person will have small and possibly irregular steps in many different directions, as if he or she is lost and trying to find his or her way. The person might fidget in his or her chair, have a shaky voice, or even have shaking or sweaty hands. You can see this type of behavior often with people who are afraid of public speaking. Most of the time they will begin with an unsteady voice and as the speech continues, they may gain the confidence that they need to make a strong finish. However, some people may never make it to that confident point in the speech, making their listeners wonder if they know what they are talking about. Their lack of confidence might make co-workers, clients, or customers question their ability to properly do their job, causing the loss of a sale or deal.

Are You Dominant?

Relative power and control of a specific interaction or relationship is known as dominance. The relative position of your body demonstrates your feelings of dominance in the relationship, whether it is personal or professional.

When one person is positioned higher than another person on the corporate ladder, it is referred to as elevation. The higher you position yourself, the more dominant you appear to the other person. When you first walk into an important meeting, you will notice that the person speaking might never sit down or that he or she is on a platform. This is done to portray that person as the one in charge; therefore, you may see him or her as the dominant force within the room. When someone wants to show that he or she is dominant over you in an office environment, he or she usually will remain standing, instead of being seated, while having a conversation.

The position of a person's hands is another indicator of dominance. When you shake hands with someone, pay close attention to how your hand is positioned. If the other person's palm is facing more toward the sky, then you appear as the dominant person. Even when you are holding the hands of your loved one, you can convey that you feel you are the dominant factor in the relationship with your body language.

When a person moves in front of another person, he or she is considered to be performing an act of dominance. This person is trying to portray that he or she is stronger than the other person — perhaps not physically, but he or she wants that person to think that. When you see a co-worker walking down the office hallway and you step in front of him or her, even if it is an accident, you are sending him or her a direct message that you think you are the dominant party. This could lead to a conflict within the office, especially if the other person believes that he or she is the dominant person.

What Is Your Status?

Dominance and status are closely related in a few areas and can sometimes be interchanged, but there are certain aspects of status that are very different from a dominant attitude. The first thing someone attempts to do to increase his or her status is increase his or her height, but there are other nonverbal cues that portray status.

Your posture is the foundation of your height, and therefore, it can be a big factor in determining your status. If you stand or sit with your back straight, shoulders pulled back, and your head up, then your body automatically becomes taller. Appearing taller as you walk or sit will not only increase your status, but it will give you a confident look.

The person who feels he or she is at a higher status will always be the person to initiate touching. This can be anything from a handshake to a pat on your back to placing a hand on your arm. Most experts agree that touch is a definite symbol of status. In a business context, when you are meeting someone for the first time, observe who is the first person to put out the hand for the initial handshake, then pay attention to the end of the conversation and see if the role switched. In the beginning of the deal, the other person might have been the one who felt he or she had a higher status, but after the conversation ended that person may not feel the same and you might feel like you have the upper hand in the situation.

Where you sit during a meeting will also convey how you think your status rates. The head of the table is generally reserved for the boss, because it is seen as the position with the highest status. The further you sit down the length of the table, away from the boss, the less likely you will be seen as having high status.

The idea of status is ingrained into us at a young age. For instance, when grandma and grandpa came to visit, you might have fought to sit next to one of them at the family dinner table. You did this because you knew you would be considered the important grandchild that particular day because you were sitting next to one of the heads of the family. Your grandparents understood the importance of this behavior, so they always made sure that each child had his or her turn when they came to visit.

Did You Catch That?

✓ Knowing your personal identity can help you change your body language to ensure success.

✓ Faking confident body language until your brain automatically registers it can help you develop the confidence you need.

✓ Darting eyes and hesitant movements will convey that you are unsure of what you are saying.

✓ Body posture, touch, and seating locations are all a part of portraying your status.

CHAPTER 17

How to Use Your Own Signals to Your Advantage

Everyone wants the raise, the promotion, and the new car, but you know that it takes time, and sometimes, it takes more time than you are willing to wait. You know that life is all about give and take, but there must be something you can do to earn your "takings" a little earlier.

Using your signals to your advantage begins with empathy; you have to place yourself in the other person's shoes to understand his or her needs. Recall a time that you were in his or her situation so will you be able to easily mirror and build a rapport with this individual. Once you have placed yourself in his or her shoes, you will be able to understand what that person's motivation is. Knowing what he or she wants will help you along your path to success because you will be able to purposely use your body language to reflect that person's motivation.

How to Seem Trustworthy

During the first ten minutes of a conversation with a complete stranger, 60 percent of people will have a tendency to lie. People also have a preprogrammed characteristic that makes them expect another person to tell the absolute truth, especially upon the first meeting. Accurately detecting the truth happens only 67 percent of the time, and detecting a lie will only happen 44 percent of the time. When you use your signals to seem more trustworthy to someone, you will make him or her want to do business with you, which might ultimately benefit him or her and you and your company.

Throughout this book, you have discovered what some of the signals of becoming trustworthy are. Encouraging feedback, listening, making direct eye contact, smiling to show your appreciation, and moving closer to a person during a conversation can indicate your trustworthiness, but there are other signs, such as keeping your feet flat on the floor, having straight posture, keeping your feet pointed toward the person your are speaking to, nodding when you are making positive points, shaking your head when you are relaying negative points, and giving the occasional submissive shrug.

To make these signals seem natural, you need to practice them. You can even practice your body language to match with your words. Try to antici-pate any question that your co-workers will have after you give your pre-sentation, or what your boss will say when you still have not completed your work, and practice your responses — both verbal and nonverbal.

Motivational Keys

When you are a manager or an executive, you need to know how to moti-vate others. Priests, politicians, and even salespeople who give speeches know the power of motivation. If you want to be a powerful figurehead, you will need to be able to motivate others to follow your lead. People will take part in marches through the middle of town so their voices can be heard on an issue that they are passionate about. This is because they know the key element to instilling change: motivation. Likewise, motivational speakers are all about instilling this same type of change — giving people the incentive they need. Often, nonverbal cues will be used by these people to create motivation.

Some of the best signals you can use to create motivation in the workplace are faster paced speech, varied pitch in your voice, and open body language, including open palms, steady eye contact, and genuine smiles. But, you have to know how to use these nonverbal signals gently and firmly at the same time. Even though you want to appear in control, you still have to give off the feeling that you care about what the other person feels. Remember that you have to put yourself in his or her shoes. If you want someone to stay late for work or do an extra assignment, then you have to motivate the person to want to do it, not strong arm him or her into doing the project.

When you are trying to motivate someone, the first thing you need to do is build rapport. After that, you should position yourself closer to the person, look him or her straight in the eye and ask for the favor you need with open palms and arms. Once you have done this, wait and see what his or her reaction is. If his or her posture becomes submissive, he or she avoids eye contact, the shoulders slump, or he or she turns away from you, then you have strong-armed the person. These are the signals that you do not want to see, so you need to rebuild rapport with that person and try motivating him or her again.

You will know when your motivational tactics have worked because you should see a look of pride with a genuine smile appear. After successfully motivating someone, he or she will feel like it was his or her idea, and will then be more than happy to take on the extra work.

Negotiations and How to Execute Them Properly

As the consumer, you have the leverage when making a big purchase, but you give up that leverage the moment your body language changes and reveals important information about you. There are salespeople out there who can tap into your nonverbal cues within 30 seconds of you entering their showroom. He or she has been paying attention to your age, sex, how you walk, your looks, your attire, what you are looking at, what you happen to look at the longest, your stance, and your smile. He or she is trying to determine what type of buyer you are, how serious you are about making a purchase, how he or she will approach you, and how he or she will motivate you into making the purchase for the highest price. If you want to retain your negotiating power, then you have to use these signals: closed posture, crossed arms, a look of indifference, closed lips, and subtle head shakes toward the salesperson. Act like you are a tough customer. Keep information about your intentions to yourself for as long as possible. Never give him or her the size of your budget or an indication of how badly you want the product he or she is selling. You are there to make a purchase, not to make a new friend. He or she will work harder with less information about you.

As the salesperson gets closer to the price you ultimately want to pay, you should open your posture, but do it slightly. Uncrossing one of your arms, and revealing a more natural face instead of a furrowed brow, will indicate that he or she is getting closer to closing this deal. If you are unsure of how this person's body language skills are, then ask him or her a few basic questions about the product. Once you have seen his or her reactions, then you will be able to begin the bargaining phase. If you are able to list a price closer to what you want and he or she tells you that it is out of the question, but his or her body language deviates, then you might have a good opportunity to get the price you want because there is a discrepancy between the body language cues and what he or she is saying.

If you are negotiating properly, then you will see extra signs. The following list outlines some from the body language cues of the salesperson that you will be able to successfully negotiate with him or her:

- Covering his or her mouth with the hands
- Fidgeting
- Biting the lip
- Placing a hand on the chest or neck
- Darting eyes
- Flushed skin
- Pacing
- Perspiring
- Picking at the lip
- Rubbing the nose
- Faster breathing.

If you wait out his or her desperation until you start to see these body language signals, you will get the price you are looking for or something within your price range.

Closing a Deal

Once you have developed a rapport, explained your product, made sure the customer knows about all of its features, and told him or her how the product can change his or her life, then you need to decide if it is the right time to close the deal. Knowing if the person is ready will be a key element in not ruining the deal after you spent all that time motivating and negotiating with that person. There are certain body language cues that you can look for to know that it is time to close the deal, such as a complete change in his or her overall body language. Smiling, enhanced eye contact, and nods of agreement will combine with open body language to show this person's willingness to take the next step.

If you see the typical "no" gestures, such as folded arms, tapping of his or her foot, placing his or her hands over his or her mouth, or eye squinting, then you cannot end your pitch there. If you get a verbal "no," then you will not close this deal at all, so it is best that you try a different approach before that "no" is said. If the client decides to think about your product, service, or company, you will get the "maybe" signs, which might include, sipping his or her drink, cleaning his or her glasses (if he or she wears any), or stroking his or her chin. All of these things provide a distraction on the client's end so he or she can side-step giving a direct commitment.

Stroking the chin portrays that you are considering an offer or contemplating what the other person is saying to you.

Making a Better First Impression

The impression you leave when you meet someone for the first time is based on your body language and the nonverbal cues you send to that person. Within the first few seconds, the other person decides if you are friendly, if you can be trusted, if you are courteous, what your status may be, and if you are confident, dominant, assertive, or aggressive. You always want to make a positive first impression, even if you woke up in a bad mood that day. You do not want that person to think you always irritable.

You might not be aware of what kind of first impression you are leaving on someone, but you would want it to be an honest first impression. But, oftentimes, an honest first impression might not satisfy what you need out of the meeting. Will that honest first impression land you the high paying job you are after? Will that honest first impression close the deal on a big account for your company? Will that honest first impression get you the sale you need in order to get the commission you so rightfully deserve?

People want instant gratification. When you first approach a person, he or she will automatically judge you. He or she does not want to work to get to know you or the best part of you; he or she wants to know who you are within the first few seconds, or minutes, of meeting you, and your body language will tell him or her everything he or she need to know.

Overcoming the first few seconds

Within one-tenth of a second, your chance at landing the big account or the high paying job might be over. The person on the other end of the interaction will make a judgment about whether you are competent. You do not even have to say so much as a "hello" before the judgment is complete. Alex Todorov, a Princeton University psychologist, is co-author of a study on snap judgments; he believes we make snap judgments because of the part of the brain that developed before a person was ever able to complete a rational thought. These judgments are made so quickly you are unable to adjust your body language, unless you are prepared for the situation.

Biting or twisting your lips can immediately turn a person off — be sure to avoid doing this during business transactions.

There are a number of actions that will immediately turn a person off to you, which will not bode well, especially if you are in need of a job or landing the major account to prove to your boss that you are worthy of that big promotion. Do not scratch your head, nervously bite or twist your lip, or raise your eyebrows incredulously. These actions will raise the suspicion that you are not sure of what you are saying. Shifting in your seat, rocking, jiggling your leg, twisting your hair, and clicking your pen will tell the other person that you are distracted. Avoid crossing your arms or displaying any other type of conceited, superior, or overbearing body language cues. Do not touch yourself, as if you are picking off invisible lint during the conversation. Biting your nails, slouching in your chair, keeping your hands in your pockets, and not using any hand gestures, along with standing rigidly in place, avoiding eye contact, and losing concentration should be avoided during the meeting or interview process. If you avoid portraying any of these nonverbal cues, then you should have no problem landing the job or account.

Tips for overcoming the snap judgment

Preparing to make a good first impression during that snap judgment involves a few steps. The first is to gather as much information about the other person as possible. This way you will know what gender he or she is, what title he or she holds within the company, and what he or she is expecting from you during this initial meeting. This information will help you to determine how you will dress, how you will greet him or her, and what nonverbal messages you intend to send within those first few crucial seconds. Try to look taller than you actually are — an erect posture will gain you a few more inches and help you exude confidence.

When you are seeking a job, new account, or new customer make sure to wear a clean, wrinkle-free suit that fits your figure well. Always go to a job interview with clean hands, fingernails, and teeth. When you are attempting to assemble your outfit, always follow the rule of less is more.

If you feel like you are overly anxious about the meeting, then you can do a few things to calm yourself down. If you get sweaty palms before an important meeting or interview, you can try two different things. One is spraying antiperspirant on your hands a few hours before to keep them from sweating, and the other is to go into the bathroom and let the cold water run over your wrists for a few seconds. This will keep your hands from sweating during the first handshake, just as long as you do not use the hand dryer after you have cooled them. To calm yourself down, you should take a few deep breaths and let them out slowly. This will slow your heart rate and force your body to relax so you do not give the impression that you are nervous about the meeting.

What happens within the first few minutes

If the person you are meeting smiles after the first few seconds, then, so far, he or she is seeing you in a positive light. You may still have your work cut out for you, though, when it comes to making that first impression last. If the person is not smiling at you, then he or she has perhaps already judged you as mistrustful, or he or she is already preparing to dislike you. You will have to double your efforts over the next few minutes to get him or her to change his or her mind. Within these next three or four minutes, your body language will begin to surface along with his or hers. The brain of both parties goes into thinking or search mode. Each person will analyze the data that he or she has already observed about the other person, such as the rate of approach, smile, handshake, proximity, smell, posture, attire, and many other details.

Making a Lasting Impression

Once you know that you have made it past the first impression, you can start to build a lasting impression. This will consist of building a rapport with your interviewer, client, or customer. Rapport is the glue that will solidify the new bond you are trying to make. You must make it all about the other person — his or her wants, needs, and expectations should all be on the forefront of your mind. Even when you are trying to sell yourself to get the job, sale, or account, you have to make sure that he or she knows you are doing him or her the favor, but do not let your body language indicate that you are being smug.

Try to maintain eye contact at least 70 percent of the time. If you fail to do so, then you might be seen as distrustful, lacking in confidence, disrespectful, or as having a short attention span. Maintaining eye contact allows the other person to see that you are confident, can be trusted, and that what he or she says is of importance to you. When you are listening to someone speak, remember to do so with your whole body. Most of the time, human tendency is to be distracted by thoughts of an appropriate response, so it is easy to not really hear what the other person is saying. Looking the other person in the eyes, nodding at the appropriate times, and tilting your head will tell him or her that you are listening to every word he or she is saying.

Also, work on eliminating distracting behaviors before you go into a meeting. Some people will jiggle their legs, click their pens, drum their fingers, or do other repetitive movements when they are nervous, distracted, or bored. You do not want to tell a client, customer, or interviewer these things about yourself, so keeping these gestures to the absolute minimum is absolutely necessary. Some people can gesture with ease, but others will over extend their gestures making them look obnoxious. If you are unsure of how your gestures look, try to avoid using them.

Putting It All Together

Not being able to articulate your feelings well does not mean that you cannot effectively communicate your needs. Eliminating a sole focus on vocal articulation can make you more perceptive and therefore make you a better communicator. When you understand body language, it can help you to perceive when a person has more to say than just what is actually being spoken.

No one wants to be judged harshly or incorrectly all the time, but it happens constantly. With the help of this book, you have learned how to overcome all of those judgments and the missteps of life to form a successful career and lasting bonds. Not only do you now have a better understanding of other people's body language, but you can also now see how you are perceived and decide how to change the things about your nonverbal cues that are stopping you from becoming a success.

Did You Catch That?

✓ Some of the best signals you can use to create motivation are characteristics of open body language: open palms, steady eye contact, genuine smiles, and mirroring body language.

✓ Keep your intentions to yourself for as long as possible when you are negotiating.

✓ Watching your client's body language at the end of your pitch will give you a hint as to whether you can close the deal or if you need to continue your pitch.

✓ Within the first few seconds of a meeting, the other person decides if you are friendly, if you can be trusted, if you are courteous, what your status may be, and if you are confident, dominant, assertive, or aggressive.

✓ Rapport is the glue that will solidify the new bond that you are making, and your body language is a powerful tool for building rapport.

APPENDIX

Open and Closed Body Language

Use these charts for a quick glance to keep your body language in check while you are at work.

NONVERBAL CLUES THAT SHOW OPEN BODY LANGUAGE:		
Body Part	*Nonverbal Cue*	*Typical Meaning*
Head	Nodding, straight ahead, sustained eye contact	Composed state, relaxed, comfortable
Arms	At sides, palms exposed, gesturing, moving in sync, rolling up sleeves, loosening attire	Comfortable, composed, relaxed
Legs	Uncrossed, parallel, relaxed, feet pointing outwards	Comfortable, composed, relaxed

NONVERBAL CLUES THAT SHOW CLOSED BODY LANGUAGE:		
Body Part	*Nonverbal Cue*	*Typical Meaning*
Head	Directing head toward something else, looking down or away from someone	Discomfort, negativity
Arms	Crossed arms in the center or folded, hands clasped or holding on to one another, holding on to body, or crossing wrists in lap	Defensiveness, negativity, discomfort, dissension
Legs	Crossed legs at ankles or knees, resting on opposite thigh, wrapping around another object, pulled away, tucked under chair or facing away from other person	Discomfort, negativity, defensiveness, dissension

BIBLIOGRAPHY

Goman, Carol Kinsey. *The Nonverbal Advantage: Secrets and Science of Body Language at Work.* San Francisco: Berrett-Koehler Publishers, 2008.

Hogan, Kevin. *The Secret Language of Business: How to Read Anyone in 3 Seconds of Less.* New Jersey: John Wiley & Sons, 2008.

Kuhnke, Elizabeth. *Body Language for Dummies.* England: John Wiley & Sons, 2007.

Pease, Allan & Barbara. *The Definitive Book of Body Language.* New York: Bantam Dell, 2004.

Reiman, Tonya. *The Power of Body Language.* New York: Pocket Books, 2007.

"Talk to the Hand: New Insights into the Evolution of Language and Gesture." *APS Observer: Association For Psychological Science* 21.5 n. pag. Web. 2010. **<www.psychologicalscience.org/observer/getArticle. cfm?id=2340>**.

"But Her Body Language Said 'Yes!'." *Newsweek* n. pag. Web. 2010. <http://blog.newsweek.com/blogs/labnotes/archive/2008/04/30/but-her-body-language-said-yes.aspx>.

"Men are hugging men more, but rules aren't always clearly defined." *Seattle P-I* n. pag. Web. 2010. <www.seattlepi.com/lifestyle/231855_guyhugs.html>.

"Changes As We Age." *Body Language University* n. pag. Web. 2010. <www.bodylanguageuniversity.com/public/193.cfm>.

"Body Language Reveals Wealth." *Live Science* n. pag. Web. 2010. <www.livescience.com/culture/090210-body-language.html>.

"What is NLP?" n. pag. Web. 2010. <www.nlpu.com/whatnlp.htm>.

BIOGRAPHY

Harmony Stalter originates from upstate New York and now makes her home in Central Florida. She is a music loving freelance writer and enjoys putting pen to paper. She discovered her love of writing at a young age and has been writing ever since. Be sure to visit her Web site at **www.harmonysfreelancewritingworld.com.**

INDEX

Direct eye contact, 106, 109-110, 119-121, 132, 148, 150, 152, 159, 164, 212, 234, 244, 250, 262

Direct manner, 182

Disagreement, 144, 229

Discomfort, 65, 199, 273

Discussion of sensitive issues, 241

Dishonest people, 61

Display of affection, 214-216

Distracting behaviors, 271

Dominance, 94-95, 119, 189, 251-252, 256-258

Double hander, 80

Dress code, 109-110, 163

E

Elbow, 74, 214-215

E-mail, 115, 146, 204, 228

Emotional distress, 188

Empathy, 261

End of a conversation, 100

Erect posture, 149-150, 165, 250-251, 269

European leg cross, 94-95

Exact indicator, 217

Executives, 48-49, 64, 75, 128, 131-132, 135, 159, 220-221, 231, 234-235, 254

Expansive movements, 221

Eye movements, 26-28, 47, 49, 56, 106, 114, 144, 217, 246-247, 250-252

Eyebrows, 52, 61, 118-119, 121, 131, 145, 157, 216, 219, 236, 268

F

Face-to-face, 123, 127

Facial expression, 26-28, 211, 226, 229, 247, 252

Facial gestures, 26-27, 246-247, 250-252

Faking confident, 255, 259

Familiar behavior, 221

Fear of rejection, 140

Fear of retaliation, 109

Fear of standing, 29-30

Feeling of happiness, 195

Feelings of insecurity, 66

Feelings of negativity, 52

Feet, 48, 93, 97, 99-101, 126, 161, 163, 166, 226-227, 250, 262, 273

Female bodies, 202

Female employee, 41, 78

Fidgeting, 23, 35, 99-100, 124, 127, 131-132, 141, 183, 229, 250, 265

Fighting stance, 227

Figure four leg clamp, 96

Fingernails, 269

Finger-pointing, 151

Fired, 30, 109, 112, 237, 239-240